Laura Garren has written a natural history of the Chattooga filled with solid science and unforgettable characters, a story as beautiful and unique as the river it describes.
—*Bronwen Dickey, daughter of James Dickey, author of* Deliverance

The CHATTOOGA RIVER

A Natural & Cultural History

Laura A Garren

Laura Ann Garren

natural
HISTORY
PRESS

Published by Natural History Press
A Division of The History Press
Charleston, SC 29403
www.historypress.net

Front cover images, clockwise from top left: Jeff Lewis, Reis Birdwhistell,
Peter McIntosh, Dr. Ed Pivorun.
Back cover images, clockwise from top left: Ethan Monk, Laura Garren, Peter McIntosh.

First published 2013

Manufactured in the United States

ISBN 978.1.60949.985.3

Library of Congress CIP data applied for.

Notice: The information in this book is true and complete to the best of our knowledge. It is
offered without guarantee on the part of the author or The History Press. The author and
The History Press disclaim all liability in connection with the use of this book.

In memory of Myra Wells Thompson

It ain't nothin' but the biggest river in the state.
—*one of the Griner brothers to Lewis in* Deliverance

Contents

Contents

Acknowledgements

I have many people to thank, but the first is Buzz Williams, whose help was invaluable. Writing this book would have been difficult, if not impossible, without him.

I also am grateful to the many people I interviewed. All were extremely generous with their time. They include Greg Borgen, Mary Bunch, Richard Cain, Kevin Colburn, Ronny Cox, Rachel Doughty, Heyward Douglass, Paul Franklin, L.L. "Chick" Gaddy, Tommy Giordano, James Glover, John Hains, Karen Hall, Nicole Hayler, Andy Hinton, Joe James, Wayne Jenkins, Drew Lanham, Caroline Lucas, David Lucas, Greg Lucas, Patrick McMillan, John Morse, Ruth Oktavek, Dan Pittillo, Scott Poore, Dan Rankin, Art Schick, Gerald Schroedl, Christopher Skelton, Skip Still, David Van Lear, Leslie White and Brad Wyche. Special thanks to Southeastern Expeditions in Clayton, Georgia, for the rafting trip; and to The American Chestnut Foundation, American Whitewater, the Chattooga Conservancy, the Foothills Trail Conference, Georgia ForestWatch, the Oconee Heritage Center, South Carolina Department of Natural Resources and Trout Unlimited.

I am grateful to Thomas Ames, Reis Birdwhistell, Karen Breedlove Chastain, Chick Gaddy, John Kilgo, Jeff Lewis, Chris Lukhaup, Peter McIntosh, Ethan Monk, Dr. Ed Pivorun and Skip Still for their beautiful photographs. Without their resonant images, I wouldn't have had a book.

I owe a huge debt of gratitude to my longtime mentor, Frank Day, for his support and benefaction. I'm grateful to Catherine Mobley, who reviewed

ACKNOWLEDGEMENTS

the manuscript and offered editorial suggestions and encouragement; and to my editor, Chad Rhoad, for his confidence in me and for his patience.

Finally, very special thanks to my husband, Charles C. (Chuck) Linnell, for being a constant source of inspiration and love.

Introduction

This book is not meant to be a detailed and comprehensive scientific inventory. My goal is to present an entertaining overview of the Chattooga River and what makes it so special. As such, I focus on what I consider the river's most interesting aspects, some of them unique. For instance, the movie *Deliverance* was filmed on the river and has had a tremendous impact, making the river a premier white-water destination that draws multitudes of people each year. The increase in use has resulted in conflict, causing some people to fear for its future; I examine ways in which they are trying to protect the river. I also examine the climate, environment, plants and wildlife of the watershed, focusing on key players and issues, as well as historical events and future challenges.

Under the Sound of the River, Birdsong

L ook back over your shoulder two hundred years. You're standing in the forest when you hear a loud rushing sound from above. Looking up through the canopy of an enormous American chestnut, you watch as the light begins to dim, the sun obscured. As the darkness descends, you start to make out distinct shapes: birds, millions of birds. They begin to land in the chestnut, so many of them that their weight breaks branches. You are surrounded by an enormous flock of passenger pigeons. This experience used to be common until the passenger pigeon fell victim to human shortsightedness and greed. What once was probably the most abundant bird in the world, according to Drew Lanham, was wiped out by overhunting. The last one died, alone in the Cincinnati Zoo, in 1914. Her name was Martha.

Lanham, a noted professor of ornithology and conservation biology at Clemson University in Clemson, South Carolina, speculates that the passenger pigeon once lived in the Chattooga River watershed. A robust bird, the passenger pigeon was the color of thick fog, with chocolate-tipped wings; a chestnut breast; Mardi Gras–purple neck feathers; and legs and eyes a startling red. Stuffed specimens stare accusingly. Their range included Canada, the U.S. East Coast from Maine to Florida, the Deep South and parts of the Midwest. Currently, the bird is the object of an effort called "The Great Passenger Pigeon Comeback," an attempt to re-create the bird using DNA and modern technology. The effort is being spearheaded by scientists from such august institutions as Harvard and Stanford. While the idea of "de-extinction" will take years of work before being tested, one day the passenger pigeon may be resurrected and may live again to darken the sky above the Chattooga River.

Another extinct avian that may have lived in the Chattooga watershed is the Carolina parakeet. Lanham imagines them in the coves, roosting in the canopy, "squealing and squawking." The only parakeet indigenous to the United States, the Carolina parakeet was green bodied, yellow headed and red cheeked. Traveling in large flocks, the birds were considered pests because they raided crops. Like the passenger pigeon, they were hunted to extinction, probably by the 1920s.

Lanham is a rare bird himself: an African American in a field that traditionally has been dominated by white men. Raised in Edgefield County, he learned to love the outdoors, pursuing a career in which he could spend a great deal of time there. He not only has reached the pinnacle of his career as a teacher and researcher but also has branched out into the literary world, writing creative nonfiction, environmental essays and poetry. He's enthusiastic and articulate, possessing an instinct for the sound bite; he has no problem hooking his listener, which serves him in and out of the classroom. But his words soar most when he talks about his passion: birds. He becomes as eloquent as a Carolina wren.

The Ivory-billed woodpecker, which requires old-growth trees and expansive deep-woods territory, is another extinct bird that might have haunted the woods of the Chattooga watershed, "a deep, dark place back then," in the nineteenth century, says Lanham. The Ivory bill, one of the largest woodpeckers in the world, was thought to have disappeared mainly due to habitat destruction. During the time that this bird was living, the Chattooga watershed was a veritable wilderness, mostly undisturbed by human activity and full of old-growth forest, both essential to the secretive woodpecker. In 2004, the scientific community and the birding world were rocked by the news that biologists had discovered a pair of Ivory bills deep in an Arkansas swamp. Although the sightings have not been verified, many people hope that the bird, caught briefly and tantalizingly on video, is an Ivory bill. The grainy image shows a large bird, black and white with a red head and a wide wingspan, demonstrating the unmistakable up-and-down, zany-looking flight pattern of a woodpecker. The "Lord-God bird" is an apt moniker for this piñata-sized bird.

The peregrine falcon narrowly missed the fate that befell its cousins. A small raptor, the peregrine became endangered in the mid-twentieth century due to the effects of the insecticide DDT, which caused the shells of its eggs to become too thin to sustain the embryo through incubation. The poison was banned in 1972, and this dainty falcon, with its dramatic black hood and speckled white breast, has made a comeback. They can be seen riding the thermals above Whiteside Mountain, where the Chattooga begins, scouting for prey.

Currently, the woods of the Chattooga watershed contain many bird species, if not passenger pigeons, Carolina parakeets and Ivory-billed woodpeckers. "For birds, rivers are natural highways," says Lanham. Specifically, the Chattooga River is "a landmark, old bird memory, because it's relatively intact," remaining much the same over millennia, from a bird's point of view. Lanham likes to imagine what the river looked like to a bird winging over an Indian village. "I can't separate the timelessness of the river from the birds. The ones that aren't there anymore, such as the passenger pigeon, and the ones there now that shared it with them," he elaborates. Birds not only connect the past to the present, he says, but also connect faraway places to each other. The scarlet tanager, for instance, connects the rivers Chattooga and Amazon. Every year, the flame-red bird with black wings migrates from Peru or Brazil, flying across the Atlantic, resting in Mexico and then traveling on to the Gulf Coast to refuel before finally making its destination, "maybe the spot where it was hatched on the Chattooga. When you hear the call of that bird, it connects you to another place." For Lanham, the most exciting time to be in the woods is when the song of a Blackburnian warbler floats down from the top of a tree. This diminutive perching bird looks like he's on the way to a masquerade party, bedecked with a black mask, jaunty black-and-white cape and orange hat and scarf.

The river creates a rich environment that acts as a net, catching birds as they migrate through—the Louisiana wood thrush or the black-and-white warbler, for instance. Many species, however, are year-round residents: chickadees, titmice and cardinals; pileated woodpeckers, downy woodpeckers and hairy woodpeckers; crows and ravens; and raptors such as red-tailed hawks and red-shouldered hawks, with an occasional osprey cruising through. Seldom seen but sometimes heard is the woodcock, also known as the timberdoodle, which makes a pipping sound as it flies upward in circles during courtship. The ruffed grouse, found nowhere else in the state, haunts the deep woods and can be heard drumming on spring mornings. Wild turkeys abound in the watershed, "except during hunting season, when they disappear!" Lanham jokes. This majestic bird, while now recovered, was hunted to critically low levels in the 1970s. However, Lanham thinks the remoteness of the watershed enabled them "to hold on in the hollers," where there were plenty of places to hide and plenty of mast to eat. He also believes that the mountain turkeys, since they have little contact with people, "have retained a real sense of their wildness."

The Chattooga River is more often than not associated with the film *Deliverance*. Based on a novel by the same name, written by James Dickey, the movie delights Lanham because "it got the birds right!" Instead of the ubiquitous loon, Carolina wrens sing lustily over the river sounds. Birds on the Chattooga have adapted to make themselves heard over the sound of the river, Lanham explains. He considers the question, what if all the birds in the world disappeared overnight? Disaster would ensue if birds were removed from the balance of life: they eat pests, pollinate and disperse seeds. On an aesthetic level, if we lost birds we would lose their infinite hues, the miracle of their flight and the beauty of their song. This scenario most likely will never happen, however. Unlike the unlucky passenger pigeon, Carolina parakeet and Ivory bill, most of the bird species of the Chattooga will continue to add their songs to the river's chorus.

You Can't Push the River

The Chattooga River begins as a drop of water falling from a rain cloud onto Whiteside Mountain. Like a tear, the drop slides down the face of a rock and trembles before splashing to the ground, where it joins other drops to form a puddle. The puddle overflows, seeping downhill, joining other seeps and forming a stream. All over the mountain, the action perpetuates. Eventually, the streams converge to form the Chattooga River, which muscles downstream for fifty-eight miles before spilling into Lake Tugalo. The Chattooga drains what is known as the Blue Ridge Escarpment, an area of sudden change in elevation in the Blue Ridge Mountains that reaches up to 4,000 feet above sea level. Referred to by the Cherokee as the Blue Wall, the escarpment constitutes the southernmost edge of the Appalachian Mountains and is composed of ancient granite sculpted by volcanic activity. Whiteside Mountain, one of the tallest in the region at almost 5,000 feet, also is considered to be one of the oldest in the world. Breast bared in 750-foot sheer cliffs, the mountain keeps watch as the Chattooga begins its improbable transformation from trickle to torrent. Draw back the curtain of time one billion years or so and you might glimpse the birth of this river, "cut by the world's greatest flood…over rocks from the basement of time," as Norman Maclean eloquently puts it. For eons, water has fallen on these mountains and coursed downhill, carving its way to the sea. There, it waits for the cycle to be repeated. Who knows how many times the same drop of water has taken this journey?

The name "Chattooga" is shrouded in as much mist as the mountains of the Blue Wall. Possibly deriving from the Cherokee word *Tsatu-gi*, it is

The Chattooga River begins as a single drop of water falling from the sky. *Photo by Reis Birdwhistell.*

thought to mean "has crossed the river" or "drank by sips," according to Georgia Genealogy Trails. *Tsatu-gi* also may have been the name of an ancient settlement located somewhere along the river. Regardless of its origins, the name "Chattooga" is widely recognized due to the fact that it is one of the premier white-water destinations in the country and the star of an iconic American movie, famous or infamous depending on whom you ask. One of the last free-flowing rivers in the Southeast, it drops one-half mile in the course of its journey and averages sixty feet wide. Much of the river corridor is primitive, thickly forested and undeveloped; it runs through Ellicott Rock Wilderness, the only area of this designation that lies in three states. Few man-made facilities are available near the river; no motorized vehicles are allowed within a quarter mile of its banks, although this rule is not strictly enforced.

In 1974, the Chattooga was designated a Wild and Scenic River by Congress, ensuring its relative protection and preservation. The Wild and Scenic Rivers Act was sponsored in 1968 by Senator Frank Church, a Democrat from Idaho, and signed by President Lyndon Johnson. The act was designed to identify and protect rivers that "possess outstandingly remarkable scenic, recreational, geologic, fish and wildlife, historic, cultural or other similar values," calling for them to "be preserved in free-flowing condition, and that they and their immediate environments shall be protected for the benefit and enjoyment of present and future generations." The Chattooga's outstanding remarkable values, or ORVs, include biology, scenery, geology, history and recreation; all flourish in this area, one of the most biologically diverse in the country.

The Chattooga's Wild and Scenic designation begins one-eighth of a mile below Cashiers Lake (North Carolina) and reaches to Lake Tugalo (South Carolina/Georgia) and includes the West Fork 7.3 miles from its confluence with the main stem of the river. Of the river's 58.7 miles, 41.6 are designated wild; 2.5 miles scenic; and 14.6 miles recreational. "Wild" refers to a river or section of river that is free of impoundment and inaccessible by trail; possessing primitive watershed and shorelines; and composed of unpolluted waters. "These represent vestiges of primitive America," according to the National Wild and Scenic Rivers System. "Scenic" rivers or sections of rivers have the same criteria, except they are accessible in some places by road. "Recreational" rivers or sections of rivers are accessible by road or railroads, may have some development along shorelines and may have had past impoundment or diversion. Further impoundment is prohibited under the act, ensuring that the Chattooga is spared the fate of so many rivers: more than seventy-five thousand large dams have modified at least 600,000 miles, or 17 percent, of American rivers. As of July 2011, 12,598 miles of 203 rivers, representing less than one-quarter of 1 percent of the nation's rivers, have been protected by the act. The statistics highlight the special nature of the Chattooga.

The Chattooga has been roughly divided, on paper, into sections. Section 00, also known as Chattooga Cliffs, runs from Grimshaw's Bridge to Bull Pen Bridge; Section 0 runs through Ellicott Rock Wilderness Area from Bull Pen Bridge to Burrell's Ford Bridge; Section 1 (formerly the West Fork), known as the Rock Gorge, runs from Burrell's Ford Bridge to the Highway 28 Bridge; Section 2, Highway 28 to Earl's Ford; Section 3, Earl's Ford to Highway 76; and Section 4, Highway 76 to Lake Tugalo. Due to its expeditious fall and circuitous flow over a streambed strewn with enormous boulders, the river has many rapids that are considered some of the best in the Southeast and include several that are rated Class 5, or extremely difficult. One set of rapids, Woodall Shoals, is rated a Class 6, which indicates risk of death.

The watershed drained by the Chattooga River is one of the most biologically diverse in the country and home to several rare plants, including

Left: The West Fork runs out of Georgia and into the main stem of the Chattooga River below the Highway 28 Bridge. *Photo by Reis Birdwhistell.*

Below: Woodall Shoals may look innocuous but is rated a Class 6 rapid. *Photo by Reis Birdwhistell.*

the Oconee bell, found nowhere else. Wildlife abounds: bears, deer, bobcats, beavers, otters, groundhogs, skunks, squirrels, chipmunks, raccoons, turtles, snakes and other such inhabitants of a southern deciduous forest roam the hills and gorges. The river is filled with fish, including (stocked) trout, as well as crawfish, frogs and salamanders. Insects scurry and buzz, birds flit and call. The climate is temperate, ranging from a low of about twenty degrees in the winter to a high of about ninety degrees during the summer, but usually not reaching those extremes. Fall temperatures are mild, normally forty to fifty degrees, sometimes higher; winter temperatures, thirty to forty degrees, occasionally lower, with infrequent incidents of snow; fifty to sixty degrees or more in the spring; and eighties to nineties in summer, which also can be very humid. Overall, however, summer temperatures are dramatically lower than those experienced at lower elevations only twenty miles away.

Rafting, kayaking, canoeing and fishing are popular activities, in addition to camping and hiking in the watershed. Three trails—the Chattooga River Trail, the Bartram Trail and the Foothills Trail—parallel the river for several miles before branching off toward their separate destinations. Due to the high rainfall and the range in elevation, many waterfalls tumble down the sides of the mountains and into tributaries that feed the river. In fact, the

Many tributaries cascade down the mountainsides and join to form the Chattooga River. *Photo by Reis Birdwhistell.*

Blue Ridge Escarpment has the highest concentrations of waterfalls in the country. Several are accessible from the Chattooga River Trail: Opossum Creek, Long Creek, Fall Creek, Licklog Creek, Pigpen, Big Bend, King Creek and Spoonauger Falls offer easy to difficult hiking experiences, but the payoff is a stunning display of water cascading over rocks into cold, deep pools before rushing away to join the Chattooga. During the summer, when water temperatures rise above seventy degrees Fahrenheit, swimming offers an invigorating occupation after a sweaty hike.

Since the river flows through three states, it is managed by three offices of the United States Forest Service: Chattahoochee National Forest in Georgia, Nantahala National Forest in North Carolina and Sumter National Forest in South Carolina. National forests, as opposed to national parks, are managed by U.S. Forest Service rangers under the Department of Agriculture and are designated multi-use "to provide Americans with a wide variety of services and commodities, including lumber, cattle grazing, mineral products and recreation with and without vehicles," according to the National Park Service. National parks, on the other hand, "emphasize strict preservation of pristine areas" and are managed by park rangers for the National Park System under the Department of the Interior. In other words, the Chattooga River lies within an area that can be logged or otherwise disturbed.

The National Forest Service was established by Congress in 1911 through the Weeks Act, which "authorized federal purchase of forestlands in the headwaters of navigable streams," according to *The Encyclopedia of American Forest and Conservation History*. Establishing national forests along rivers made logging easier because these waterways made good highways for timber. These lands already had been logged out in places and over-farmed in others; they were called the "Lands Nobody Wanted," so the federal government bought them for as little as five dollars per acre. Until the late 1880s, federal policy had been to sell the public domain, placing millions of acres of land in the hands of private landowners. The U.S. Forest Service now manages 193 million acres of national forests and grasslands.

The first ten miles of the Chattooga run through North Carolina. This portion of the river is managed by the Nantahala Ranger District of the Nantahala National Forest, which is composed of 531,148 acres. The remaining forty-eight miles of the river form the border between South Carolina and Georgia, terminating in Lake Tugalo. Until 1923, when the lake was created by the construction of a dam, the water continued to flow and eventually joined the Savannah River. On the South Carolina side, the river is managed by the Andrew Pickens Ranger District of Sumter National

Forest, which oversees 85,000 acres. The Chattooga District, part of the 261,035-acre Chattahoochee-Oconee National Forest, manages the river from the Georgia side.

As noted, while the Chattooga River itself is protected, the forests in the watershed are subject to logging or other activities by the National Forest Service. Before any proposed action can be taken, however, the Forest Service is required by the National Environmental Policy Act to conduct an environmental impact statement (EIS), sounding as if the agency seeks outside expertise. However, the Forest Service both conducts the EIS and then makes a decision based on its own results, a situation reminiscent of a fox guarding the henhouse. Next, the Forest Service must publish a notice of intent (NOI) in the *Federal Register* and solicit public input, as directed in the 2012 "National Forest System Land Management Planning Rule." But not everyone wants to read the *Federal Register*, a ponderous, daily tome full of obfuscating legal jargon. So how does the public find out what the Forest Service is planning? One way is to become involved with any number of environmental watchdogs, whose mission is to protect the chickens from the foxes, so to speak. These overseers—the Chattooga Conservancy and Georgia ForestWatch being two prominent local environmental entities— publish newsletters, call for action, raise funds and awareness, file lawsuits and try to prevent exploitation of natural resources.

Another way to procure information involves perseverance and can result in extreme frustration, as the process involves many steps and is fraught with misdirection. First, direct an Internet browser to the "Forest Service NEPA (National Environmental Policy Act) Projects" website. Under each of four headings, a drop-down tab reading "Select a Forest" contains a list of forests under consideration for the respective headings: NEPA Projects, SOPA (Schedule of Proposed Actions), Appeal Responses and Objection Responses. If you want to see if any SOPAs might affect the Chattooga River in South Carolina, you will have to remember to click "Francis Marion and Sumter National Forest" on the drop-down tab. The next page will be "Forest Service Schedule of Proposed Actions for the Francis Marion and Sumter National Forests," and a few lines down you will be directed to "Click to view the current SOPA report." A separate window opens, and from there you can click on the appropriate link, in this case, "Francis Marion and Sumter National Forests, Andrew Pickens Ranger District."

You then will see a chart with the name, purpose, planning status, decision, expected implementation and contact listed for each proposed project. If you want to find out more about, say, the "AP Loblolly Pine Removal and

Restoration Project" under consideration at the time of this writing, click on the web link to be directed back to the Forest Service website, to a page titled "AP Loblolly Pine Removal and Restoration Project." Under Project Documents, see "Scoping" and click the PFD file "Scoping_Letter_AP_ LP2-26-10." Up pops a letter from the ranger station at the Andrew Pickens District of Sumter National Forest, describing the proposed project in eleven pages of detail. Page two provides contact information so that you, should you get this far, have the opportunity to comment per NEPA regulation. Thus, the Forest Service fulfills its charge to provide "an opportunity for the public to be involved in the Federal agency decisionmaking [sic] process." It seems fair to appropriate Winston Churchill's quote about Russia, which he called "a riddle wrapped in a mystery inside an enigma."

Government agencies may be enigmatic, but the attraction to the Chattooga River certainly is no mystery. This priceless resource offers endless opportunities for exploration, wilderness experience, beauty, solitude and challenge. The gift keeps renewing itself, one raindrop at a time.

Deep Like the River

You can't have a meaningful conversation about the Chattooga River without mentioning Buzz Williams's name, because he arguably is the most avid watchdog who has ever guarded the river. He spearheaded one of the most dedicated grassroots efforts to champion a cause, forming an advocacy group to protect the Chattooga River in 1991. Much like the river's journey from trickle to torrent, the organization started small and grew into what now is known as the Chattooga Conservancy.

Williams lives not far from the river, in Clayton, Georgia. He's sixty-ish, tall and lean with a shock of graying blond hair falling over his forehead. His gaze penetrates sharply through slightly smudged glasses, and he's trailed by the faint, pleasing odors of wood smoke and water. His expression, when lit with a smile, is warm and engaging, especially when he talks about the Chattooga. However, when he discusses the dangers facing the river, lines of concern crease his face. He is passionate about the river, balancing between hope and despair about its future.

His love affair with the Chattooga began at an early age, when he took to the forest in the Chattooga River watershed because it was the most remote place he could go out and experience nature. He was born and raised in Pendleton, South Carolina, about a forty-five-minute drive from the river, which he visited often and which became his "solace, a place to go to seek solitude, challenge, risk, adventure." These qualities later won the Chattooga the Wild and Scenic River designation, but Williams enjoyed them from a very early age; a seed was planted. As he grew older, Williams traveled all over the world, looking for the most remote

Buzz Williams and his daughter Jasmine run Surfin'
Rapid. *Photo by Sarah D. McWhirt.*

places he could find. In time, he realized that he had "one of the most special wild places right in my backyard." The seed sprouted.

After attending college at Clemson University, where he majored in forestry, Williams went to work for the Forest Service. Fairly early in his career, he realized he didn't like the agency's way of doing business in the forests it had been charged to protect. "The timber that had been devastated at the turn of the [nineteenth] century was recovering, and they [the Forest Service] went in with a vengeance," he relates. Disturbed by this lucre-driven philosophy, Williams helped start a group called the Association of Forest Service Employees for Environmental Ethics, which joined the frontlines of the fight to save the remaining 4 percent of the Pacific Northwest old-growth forest, home of the spotted owl. Under public scrutiny and pressure, the Forest Service finally promised to change the management paradigm to a more environmentally sensitive one.

The sprout began to grow. Williams decided to "come home to fight for my own backyard," using what he had learned to stop the Forest Service's logging and road-building incursions into the Chattooga River watershed. To aid his efforts, in 1991 he founded the Chattooga River Watershed Coalition with the late Dr. Robert Zahner, professor emeritus of forestry at Clemson University. Zahner was on the coalition's board and was instrumental in convincing the Forest Service to use the Chattooga River watershed as a pilot project for a new, ecologically sensitive way of handling resources. The coalition became a monitoring organization to ensure that the agency used its data correctly and followed through with its responsibilities. Williams, as executive director, burst into action, oak-strong and ready to take on the establishment.

The mission of the coalition, now the Chattooga Conservancy, is "to protect, promote and restore the natural ecological integrity of the Chattooga River watershed ecosystems; to ensure the viability of native species in harmony with the need for a healthy human environment; and, to educate and empower communities to practice good stewardship on public and private lands." In 1995, the conservancy opened an office in Clayton, Georgia, as it gained support and funding. According to its website, it plays "a pivotal role in the Forest Service's ecosystem management project by providing much critical oversight and input…" and helps "advance a paradigm change in the Forest Service's management philosophy, towards ecosystem management." The organization also helped create the Chattooga Conservation Plan, one of the first watershed restoration plans in the East, with Clemson University, the Conservation Fund and the Southern Appalachian Forest Coalition.

The conservancy continues to monitor the Forest Service's management of the watershed, recently opposing a plan to develop 20 acres of riverside property into a theme park. In 1970, the Forest Service bought the site of the old Russell House, which burned in 1988, along with 187 acres of land located within the Wild and Scenic River corridor near the Highway 28 Bridge. According to the conservancy, the proposed project would include: reducing stream buffers from one hundred to forty feet; constructing a thirty-car parking lot within two hundred feet of the Chattooga; building a gift shop; installing livestock pastures and corrals, as well as additional buildings; clearing trees; and using herbicides. The property would be leased to the Oconee Heritage Center, which would be charged with the management of the development, the "Southern Appalachian Homestead," and would be allowed to charge admission and to use the property for fundraising events.

The Wild and Scenic River Act is called on to "protect and enhance the values" that cause a river to be designated; "primary emphasis shall be given to protecting its esthetic, scenic, historic, archaeologic, and scientific features." Clearly, the development of a theme park would violate this standard, so the Forest Service engaged in some revision, proposing amendments to the Sumter National Forest Plan that would allow development inside the Wild and Scenic River corridor, according to the conservancy. Reduction of the stream buffer would allow sediment to drain into the river, which would negatively impact fish and other aquatic species, not to mention the fishermen; a trout-stocking area is located not far upstream from the proposed site. In addition, the land is adjacent to the site of an old Cherokee village, Chattooga Town. In response to the Forest Service's proposal, the conservancy issued an action alert, calling for Friends of the National Wild and Scenic River to contact the Forest Service and denounce the plan. Williams says that the response was enormous. As a result, the Oconee Heritage Center withdrew its request to the Forest Service for a special use permit for the property.

The conservancy also opposes a Forest Service plan to remove thousands of acres of nonnative loblolly pine and replace them with native pine and hardwood, claiming that the plan also calls for: herbicide use; the logging of six thousand acres; the reconstruction of almost sixty miles of roads and the construction of twelve new roads; and, in short, the planting of "more pine plantations." Throwing up obstacles for the Forest Service is not the only function of the conservancy, however. The agency offered alternative changes to the plan, including the employment of landscape science based on soil type, slope and other features; the use of restoration techniques that will ensure the return of true native species; the performance of a cost-benefit analysis to demonstrate the expenses involved in a loblolly removal plan; and management of existing roads as opposed to the construction of new ones.

The most recent conflict has arisen over a plan to erect a cellphone tower in the watershed. While the tower would be built on private property, it would be within sight of the river, as well as that of adjacent landowners. The conservancy opposes this incursion of modern life into the wild and scenic Chattooga River corridor. Obviously, a cellphone tower looming over the river would defeat the purpose of a wilderness experience. Williams also has focused conservancy efforts on the restoration of Stekoa Creek, in Clayton, which is one of the most polluted tributaries of the Chattooga. In addition, he is overseeing the restoration of native cane in a bottomland near the Russell House and Chattooga Town. The project is supported by a grant from the Cherokee Preservation Association, and the cane will be ready for harvest by the Cherokee in five to six years. Standing on the edge of a large, open field, Williams indicates a small mound that once was the council house of the tribe that lived in Chattooga Town. Cane, he explains, was the Indians' number two crop, after corn, and was used for making baskets, spear shafts and other weapons. "This cane is blowgun ready," he says, running his hand over a mature stalk. Cane, which was displaced by farmers, resembles bamboo and, like bamboo, is a grass. Found in flood plains and along the banks of streams, cane was interspersed with riparian trees and composed about 30 percent of the vegetation.

The conservancy, now headed by Williams's wife, Nicole Hayler, publishes a newsletter called the *Chattooga Quarterly*, which features articles about the watershed's natural and cultural assets, as well as updates readers about activities. The conservancy also works to raise public awareness through outreach and education. And now that he is no longer constrained by his role as head of the organization, Williams is free to fight for the continued protection of the river he loves, which seems likely to last as long as there's a river to fight over.

The Country of Nine-Fingered People

In 1972, a star burst upon the national scene. From relative obscurity, this new celebrity was thrust into the limelight with the release of the hit film *Deliverance*, based on the novel of the same name by James Dickey. Suddenly, people were aware of this national treasure, swarming from all over the country to get a glimpse of the reclusive celebrity. The player (one might argue, the star) was the Chattooga River, as much of a presence in the film as the actors who portrayed the four hapless suburbanites who undertake a "man-versus-nature adventure" and instead descend into hillbilly hell. They pay incalculably. One loses his life.

The doomed character is Drew; the actor who portrays him, Ronny Cox. The other players were Burt Reynolds as Lewis, Jon Voight as Ed and Ned Beatty as Bobby. In a telephone interview, Cox reminisces about his experience on the river during the making of what has become an iconic American movie. "It was my first film, my first big break," he says. But, he adds, it was "so unlike making a film. It was sort of like being on a Boy Scout adventure." He recalls being impressed by the beauty of the Chattooga, even as he jokes, "It was a prop!" Incidentally, when his friends find Drew, his arm has been horribly twisted around the back of his own neck—not a prop. Cox actually was able to dislocate his own shoulder and sling it over the opposite shoulder.

Cox has visited the river since the release of the film, performing with his band there in 2012 at the fortieth-anniversary *Deliverance* celebration in Clayton, Georgia, where the movie people stayed. Cox, who performed

"Dueling Banjos" for the famous scene between Drew and the banjo-picking boy, is a true musician as well as a gifted actor. At a house concert at the home of a friend in Asheville, North Carolina, Cox warmly welcomes all visitors at the door. He then sits down for a couple of hours and proceeds to sing, play guitar and tell funny stories. During an intermission, he chats with people and signs CDs. Accompanied by two other musicians, Cox sings several songs written by himself, as well as several folk classics. He does not perform "Dueling Banjos," although he confides that his band sometimes does play what he calls a "corrupted version." Neither did he play the tune in the movie, but he did simulate the fingering of each note. The banjo boy, played by Billy Redden, still lives in Clayton; Cox has seen him a couple of times since the film was released.

After the movie exploded into the American consciousness, James Dickey famously expressed regret about his perceived degradation of the Chattooga as a result of *Deliverance*. He had written a brilliant, bestselling novel, which is on one level a lament for a damned river. In the wake of its success, Dickey realized a tragic irony in the movie, believing it diminished what he called the river's "wildness." Cox echoes these sentiments, saying, "All of us felt that way, because it was so pristine." While the business of making the movie was "a boon to the area economically, on the other hand, we sort of spoiled a beautiful river." While the Chattooga was shortly thereafter assured protection as a National Wild and Scenic River, Cox frets, "It's still not the wild river that it was."

Dickey, perhaps foreseeing potential overexposure of the Chattooga, originally wanted the location of the film to be a river in Florida, Cox says. However, Director John Boorman and his people found the Chattooga, and the rest is movie history. Because Dickey's novel had been a bestseller, Cox explains, "Everyone knew it [the film] was going to be big. Every actor in Hollywood wanted to be in that film." Boorman wanted the story to be the most important element, so he decided against casting well-known actors who would make too big a splash, so to speak. Instead, he chose actors whose stars had not yet risen, although they certainly did so after they played the main roles in this film. *Deliverance* tells the story of four paddling neophytes who decide to run a river that has been slated for damming. The "leader" of the group is Lewis, played by Reynolds, who is hypermasculine. While capable, Lewis has fallen under the delusion that many competent, cocky men do: that, since he is good at most things, he is simply invincible. Why else would he toss two canoes—one of them wooden—into a boulder-strewn white-water river without any knowledge, preparation or experience?

Because it's wild, he says in the novel, "and I *mean* wild; it looks like something up in Alaska." The other three men, generally contented with their lives but still needful of manly pursuits, trustfully follow Lewis. They pay dreadfully for his hubris and lack of respect for the river.

Another aspect of the film that attracted, yet repelled, was the rape scene. Not only was the act shocking (the year, remember, was 1972), but it also generated a lot of animosity on the part of southerners in general and Georgians in particular, especially Clayton locals. In it, two mountain men are depicted as sodomizing rednecks. However, the scene, Cox says, was "beautifully choreographed, almost like dance," and featured stellar work by Beatty and character actor Bill McKinney, who played his attacker. (Myth holds that Beatty was so traumatized by the experience that he never would discuss the scene, but Cox dispels the rumor.) Many people overlooked the skill of the players and the artistry of the scene, focusing on and resenting what they thought of as stereotypes of themselves. As Cox points out, "There are heroes and villains everywhere. If you made a film in Texas with two bad men, you wouldn't think that everyone in Texas is bad." Besides, he adds, *Deliverance* portrayed more decent people than bad ones: the man and boy at the gas station, the folks around the dinner table at the end of the film and the little banjo-playing boy. The Griner brothers, who transport the men's cars down to the takeout point, are honest if not hospitable. But who can blame them? They are patronized and mocked by the city men (although not by the genial Drew), who make fun of their accents and laugh at the old man who cuts capers

The road leading to deliverance. *Photo by Reis Birdwhistell.*

during "Dueling Banjos." They endure Lewis's arrogance and recklessness as he careens down a dirt road toward the river, refusing to let them show him the way.

Unlike the characters they played, Cox and his fellow actors knew how to paddle their canoes; the director arranged for the men to be rigorously instructed before he began filming. Among other experiences, they had to swim through rapids so that they would know what to do if they capsized. "We had to learn to survive, how to get through if you fall out, which was going to happen," and did, says Cox. In fact, both he and Beatty had near-drowning experiences when they each got caught in a hydraulic. They did, however, successfully run Bull Sluice and Woodall Shoals, which have taken more lives than any other stretch of river.

Cox describes many more movie-making experiences in his book *Dueling Banjos: The Deliverance of Drew*, published in 2012. The book is a compilation of his memories, related conversationally, regarding his experiences and the people involved. In one chapter, he states *Deliverance* is one of the few films he's liked as much as the novel, even though the experiences of reading and viewing are so different. While novels are "an intellectual exchange between the author and the reader," film is "a visceral and a visual experience," sometimes simultaneously. Through the artistry of John Boorman, the adaptation of the novel succeeds brilliantly as a film, even decades later. Cox says that many people miss the artistic sensibility of it because it's so harrowing. Knowing what's going to happen only heightens the sense of menace, even as the river burbles merrily. Multiple viewings can't quite dispel the tension of watching the four men paddle down the river to their reckoning. They don't hear the banjos.

Death on the River

No murderous hillbilly attacks have occurred on the Chattooga River, at least not on record. However, forty-two people have lost their lives on the river since the Forest Service began keeping records of fatalities in 1970, according to the agency. Of those, fifteen were drowned in the three years following the movie *Deliverance*. Eight occurred at particularly hazardous spots, four each at Bull Sluice and Woodall Shoals. Only one of these victims was wearing a personal floatation device (PFD), and one individual was running Bull Sluice on an inner tube. Considering that hundreds of thousands of people have used the Chattooga since 1970, the fatality rate is low—an annual average of two. However, the river's currents are very strong in some places and can overwhelm the careless, inexperienced or unlucky. To complicate the matter, the water level can change quickly and transform the river from placid to perilous. Ultimately, people must wade, swim or boat at their own risk, but the potential for injury or death may be minimized with certain precautions and a healthy dose of respect.

People underestimate water, which is understandable. After all, you can scoop it up in your hands, swim through it and make it conform to almost any shape. You can even transform it from liquid to steam or ice. "People can't imagine how powerful water is because it's so alien to a land-dwelling primate," says John Hains, a professor at Clemson University. His specialty is limnology, the study of lakes and rivers, and he uses the term "stream" to refer to free-flowing water. Other names for a river include creek, kill, lick and run. These designations don't reveal much about the actual entity and simply are social constructs.

Of the forty-two fatalities that have occurred on the river from 1970 to 2013, the Forest Service reports that thirteen people were not wearing PFDs. However, wearing a PFD is no guarantee that you won't drown; six people who lost their lives in the river were wearing PFDs that were ripped off by the force of the current. It is not known if these were correctly adjusted. Another demonstration of the power of moving water is the fact that twenty people, some of them experienced boaters, drowned as a result of being pinned or otherwise entrapped; seven others became trapped but escaped or were rescued. In one case, a kayaker stepped into a hole in a rock where his foot became stuck; the force of the water bent his body over. The water flowed over him with such force that he was unable to pull himself upright in fairly shallow water, and he drowned.

At least six people drowned swimming or wading—including one person who didn't know how to swim and one who was intoxicated—after being caught in powerful currents and swept downstream. At least two victims remained trapped in a hydraulic for several days or longer, as in the case of fifteen-year-old Rachel Trois in 1999. According to the Forest Service report, on May 29, Rachel, who was not wearing a PFD, attempted to wade across the river near Raven Rock Rapid. She lost her footing and was swept downstream, where she disappeared into the rapid and never surfaced. A major effort was overtaken to retrieve her body, and after a dam was constructed to divert the waters and facilitate recovery, divers were able to swim into the rapid. There, they found some of Rachel's clothing tangled in a log. She apparently was swept into the rapid, trapped by the hydraulic effect and drowned. The river finally released her body after it disintegrated, and not until July 28 were her remains finally recovered, about thirty feet farther downstream.

Hains describes the mechanics of getting caught in a hydraulic, starting with an explanation of "kinetic, the theme that organizes the whole entity. When a stream flows, it has mass. It obeys the laws of gravity, and when it moves, it creates friction along the streambed." A hydraulic is created when the water flows in a predictable pattern. Hydraulic action can produce gentle eddies, in which a boater can rest before paddling back into the current; or it can create a potentially life-threatening condition, as in the notorious Bull Sluice. What makes Bull Sluice so treacherous is a combination of factors. First of all, the river is being squeezed through a narrow passage, as opposed to spread out over a large surface; the force of the water is greater because

Above: Bull Sluice at low water. *Photo by Peter McIntosh.*

Below: Bull Sluice at flood stage. *Photo by Peter McIntosh.*

as the channel narrows, its velocity increases. Second, as the water rockets through this space, it drives hard against the bottom of the riverbed and into a deep hole that has been gouged out over eons. Once something enters, it sometimes stays for a while; the action that causes this phenomenon is called a hydraulic. The combination—of water moving swiftly through a narrow passage and churning relentlessly in a deep hole—can be very dangerous, especially if the water level is high.

Twenty-eight people have drowned in the Five Falls area, which consists of five harrowing bursts of white water: the Entrance, Corkscrew, Crack-in-the-Rock, Jawbone and Sock-em-Dog. Crack-in-the-Rock alone is the site of six deaths. Woodall Shoals has taken seven lives and the Narrows, four. By far, Bull Sluice is considered by some to be the most challenging and dangerous rapid, having caused eleven deaths. The water plunges over and around a set of enormous boulders, and the final cascade crashes down and curls in a small but turbulent concentration. A raft can fold virtually in half, shutting like a clam, as its front end shoots over the rapid, slams into the hydraulic and pops out of the water to meet its back end. While this rapid and others on the Chattooga are not for the inexpert boater, the Bull's notoriety may be exaggerated. Andy Hinton points out that part of the reason for these many deaths is that Bull Sluice is very accessible, as is Woodall Shoals. "The more people who are on the river, the higher the incidence of death," he says. Hinton is the river operations manager at Southeastern Expeditions, a rafting outfitter that guides river trips.

If you watch YouTube footage of rafters and kayakers on the Chattooga, you will detect a dollop of macho flippancy. Most of the boaters are young males, and their seemingly careless attitudes imply a lack of respect for the river, or perhaps just denial. "I'll never drown," they think. "That will never happen to me." However, probably anyone who's boated on the Chattooga thinks they'll survive; otherwise, they probably wouldn't take the risk. One video features the voices of young men woo-hooing as they watch a raft hit the bottom of Bull Sluice, buckle in the middle and violently eject its occupants. "Dude, Where's My Boat" features a paddler who flips out of his kayak seconds before both boater and boat shoot over Bull Sluice. The paddler emerges downstream, unharmed, but witnessing the incident is hair-raising in this clip subtitled "What NOT to do on the infamous rapid Bull Sluice." Another video shows a raft getting stuck at the base of Sock-em-Dog, where it is pummeled by white water as one paddler struggles to dislodge it and the others tumble out and swim away. Most of these videos also feature frenetic rock music, as if simply watching weren't enough to excite the adrenal glands.

During the first three years of record keeping, the Forest Service did not report the names, ages or genders of the four recorded drowning victims. However, of the fatalities thereafter, fourteen were young men between the ages of fifteen and twenty-five. The oldest was sixty-four-year-old Ralph Head, who drowned after becoming entangled in the undercut of a rock after his canoe capsized. The youngest victim was ten-year-old Brittani Briones, who drowned after being swept off her feet while attempting to wade across the river.

Drowning is not the only danger to be encountered on the river. At least two people have died of exposure, or hypothermia, including twenty-five-year-old paddler Mark Hinz, who was the victim of a freak accident. He was not even in his boat but standing in waist-deep water when the wind knocked loose a tree branch, which fell on and pinned him. The month was March, so the water was very cold, probably around 47.0 degrees Fahrenheit (15.6 Celsius). Hypothermia occurs when the body's temperature drops from the normal 98.6 degrees to 95.0 or colder, according to Minnesota Sea Grant. Hypothermia can cause symptoms as mild as shivering but in extreme cases will progress to numbness, confusion, slurred speech, unconsciousness, weak or no pulse, bluish-gray skin, diluted pupils and rigidity of the muscles. Death can result.

The colder the water, the faster the onset of hypothermia, but the real risk starts in water lower than 60.0 degrees. If a person falls into water between 50.0 and 60.0 degrees, he might be able to withstand submersion for one to two hours before becoming unconscious; survival time ranges from one to six hours. If the water is 40.0 to 50.0 degrees, survival time would be one to three hours; for water 32.5 to 40.0 degrees, thirty to ninety minutes; at 32.5 degrees, forty-five minutes. Survival times vary according to a person's age, fitness and health; intoxication can speed the process. Interestingly, wearing a PFD, especially the vest variety, increases survival time by providing significant insulation—another good reason to strap one on. Treatment for mild to moderate hypothermia includes warming the victim and offering him warm liquids, if he is fully conscious. For more severe cases, keep the victim warm; obtain medical assistance; ignore the victim if he says he doesn't need help; elevate the feet; and give CPR, but only if there is no breathing or pulse. Never assume the victim is not revivable.

The average water temperature of the Chattooga varies greatly from month to month; January's water is the coldest. According to the United States Geological Survey (USGS), the mean for January (2009–11) was 37.0 degrees. The month having the warmest mean water temperature during that same period was August, at 70.7, which still is far below what is considered the ideal water temperature of about 80.0 degrees. If you are average in weight, age and health and you fall in the water during January through March, you might last an hour before succumbing to hypothermia; April and May, three hours; June through September, you might be safe from hypothermia, even though the water still is far from warm; October through December, you'll last a couple of hours.

Another risk variable arises with the water level, which can fluctuate very dramatically, very quickly, during a rainstorm. One YouTube video features a clip of Bull Sluice during flood stage. Normally, this rapid is considered challenging, a "mandatory scout" and possibly the greatest moment of the run, reports the Chattooga River Wild and Scenic River website. Green water spills gracefully over an impressive drop in the rocks, churning into white foam before re-forming itself into a green ribbon and continuing downstream. In flood stage, however, the Bull transforms into an angry brown monster with massive, toothy white waves engulfing the normally visible rocks. Considering that most of the drowning deaths occurred when the water level was low—between one and two feet—it's easy to see that high levels could result in extremely treacherous conditions. The Forest Service reports that a twenty-year-old man who, along with four friends, had little or no white-water experience attempted to raft the river after a "twenty-five-year storm event" that produced a flood level of ten feet (commercial outfitters suspend rafting trips if the water level is higher than four and a half feet). The raft flipped at Dick's Creek, and the man's body was found at Sandy Ford, almost a mile downstream, two days later. Although he had been wearing a PFD, it was ripped from his body and found elsewhere.

As noted, the annual rate of fatalities is very low considering how many people use the river each year. If you plan on boating and you lack experience, first gain the necessary proficiency on still water, or go with one of the three outfitters that offer rides. Find out the water temperature and wear a wet suit when the danger of hypothermia is present. If you do know what you're doing, take precautions: check the flood level, scout the rapids and wear a helmet (which is required in some sections anyway). And whether you're boating, swimming or wading, advises the Forest Service, always wear a PFD. Don't become one of the agency's statistics.

The point is that whenever you step into the Chattooga, caution is necessary. Even then, risk is involved; after all, water is a powerful, unpredictable force that demands respect. Withhold it at your peril.

Go Play in the Water

The raft plunges over the frothing rapid, eliciting screams and soaking everyone aboard. The guide, positioned in the back of the raft where he can steer, instructs the passengers to keep paddling so they can rest in an eddy and wait for the others. The current is stronger than it looks, and the five riders strain forward and apply their paddles. Then, dripping and happy, they share reactions to the experience and express relief and satisfaction that no one in their group fell out. Their luck and determination hold throughout the day as they float Section 4 of the Chattooga. None of them goes swimming, at least not involuntarily.

Before beginning, they gather with a group of others at the office of Southeastern Expeditions in Rabun County, Georgia, on Highway 76, just a couple miles from the river. The Chattooga River Outpost is a rustic wooden structure featuring a covered porch lined with benches; a deck with men's and women's showers and hangers full of waterproof slipovers for guests; a stairway leading to toilets; a gift shop; and a small room used for pre-rafting instruction and a post-rafting slide show. Guests sit on benches lining the walls while a guide tells them what to expect and what is expected of them. They must wear PFDs, helmets and proper shoes and be aware that a very real danger of injury, even death, exists. While drownings happen very infrequently, they have occurred on the river during these kinds of trips.

Finally, time to go. Everyone climbs into an ancient school bus that has seen better days. The backs of the seats are bleeding foam, and sitting in one brings back "the inexorable sadness of pencils" during "long afternoons of tedium," as recalled by Theodore Roethke in "Dolor," his lugubrious poem about school. Spitballs, thumps on the head, the sour smell of old milk and the sweat of children, the sounds of cursing, shouting and laughter haunt the dusty interior of the yellow time capsule. Thankfully, the ride lasts only a couple minutes. Then everyone unloads, gears up and walks down to the river to begin the five-hour rafting adventure. The air is warm, the water is cold and the sun shines weakly through the clouds as each raft pushes off, bearing five to six passengers and an expert guide.

Southeastern Expeditions is one of three commercial outfitters operating on the river and also offers kayak and canoe clinics and overnight camping trips. Starting in March, Southeastern runs four trips per day on weekdays and one per day on Saturdays and Sundays. "We under-strip our limits on weekends to make way for private boaters," says Andy Hinton, who adds that the three outfitters stagger their trips so that they don't bump into each other. The season lasts until October or November, depending on how long people want to go rafting. Kayakers and other private boaters continue to run the river all winter, which is the best time according to Hinton, river operations manager for the outfitter. "There is a lot of rain, and the trees are dormant, so the ground gets saturated and the water table goes up," producing high water levels, he says.

Today, high water makes the trip very exciting. In addition to the twenty-five guests, six staff members are along—one for each of the three rafts and three in kayaks. Two of the kayakers scout ahead to check out each of the rapids, weighing thrill against risk. They also set up rescue ropes, suspended between rocks on either side of the river, in the event anyone gets "tossed." In this case, the guests have been instructed what to do before that particular rapid: swim left or right or look for a rescue rope, and always keep feet pointed up to prevent entrapment. The third kayaker positions himself on a rock to take photographs of each raft as it descends each rapid. Later, back at the office, he displays his shots and burns CDs for guests to take home. Everyone gets a laugh seeing the expressions on faces as the rafts crash down a rapid: mouths open in fear or excitement, jack-o'-lantern grins when it's over and they've made it.

Hinton decides what section to raft based on the water level, which is monitored by a United States Geological Survey (USGS) gauge from the bridge on Highway 76 (Georgia/South Carolina). "People who use the river for boating are familiar with how the water level changes at that reference point and what effect it has on different parts of the river," he explains. Some of the rapids become more powerful in higher water, making them harder to negotiate from both rafting and rescuing standpoints. The consequences increase with the water level, which is why at four and a half feet, commercial trips are suspended. "Not much stopping if you have any accidents. The current is up the bank, into the trees," adds Hinton, a bearded, attractive thirty-something with a ponytail and soulful eyes. On the other hand, if the river is low, he employs smaller rafts and loads them with fewer people.

Meanwhile, back on the river, the guides set up their rescue positions on rocks. The rafts are beached upstream against a rocky outcrop. The damp guests warm themselves in the sun. Suddenly someone exclaims, "Look at that!" and points to a banded water snake undulating through the water, a small fish gripped in its mouth. As everyone rushes toward it, the startled snake changes course and swims downstream a bit farther. If a snake could have a surprised expression, this one would as the knot of curious onlookers follows it downstream. Finally, the snake escapes into a crack in a rock, no doubt relieved, where he can eat his meal in peace. Soon the guests are treated to a lunch of their own, a picnic of sliced meats, cheese, bread, condiments, chips, fruit and cookies. The exertion of paddling and the chill of being waterlogged heighten appetites. The water temperature is about sixty-five degrees, not warm enough to invite swimming but not cold enough to discourage anyone from climbing a thirty-foot rock and then leaping off. The freefall is followed by a wet slap, an icy shock and a bracing swim against the current. Everyone, from the young married couple to the sixty-something man, takes the plunge and, upon surfacing, gives a shriek or shout of joy. The guides wait watchfully from rafts, ready to rescue anyone who needs it.

River guides, sometimes known as river rats, traditionally are males, average age between eighteen and twenty-four. However, last season, almost half the hires were women, indicating a trend toward gender equality for river rats. Male or female, says Hinton, he looks for people who are fit, have white-water experience and a strong work ethic and spend days off pursuing physical activities as opposed to "sitting around drinking beer and telling stories." The job may seem like a rugged, romantic occupation, and maybe it is, but it also carries heavy responsibilities. First, a guide must keep a raft full of people safe. Second, he must also be "a people person," Hinton explains: "I can teach a monkey to guide a raft. I can't teach a monkey to sit in the back of a raft all day and be pleasant to strangers." To that end, he recruits guest speakers to give weekly presentations during the season so his guides can learn river tidbits to share with guests.

Tommy Giordano represents the ideal guide, chatting up the guests in his raft, pointing out interesting landmarks such as Deliverance Rock. Named for the place where the crew of *Deliverance* lost thousands of dollars' worth of camera equipment, the rock juts mockingly over a deep pool. After the snake sighting, someone asks Giordano about the most interesting thing he's seen on the river. With a grin and no hesitation, he describes watching an otter playing with its next meal, in this case, a snake. But watching a mother Canada goose and her goslings swim down Woodall Shoals, a Class 6 rapid, was most amazing and comical, he adds. (Interestingly, no one seems to be able to explain the names of all the rapids. While some rapids are so named for obvious reasons—Deliverance Rock, for example—the roots of others don't seem to be recorded or agreed upon.) Since the job of river guide is seasonal, not many guides stick around for long, on average two or three seasons. Some move on to other rivers, some go back to school, some enter the "real" workforce. Hinton admits that it's hard to see them go, especially when they've become knowledgeable and expert, but he accepts this part of the job and encourages them to move on when ready. "It's not a career for most people," he admits, although he is an exception, having worked at Southeastern since 1997.

As the rafts continue downstream to lower elevation, the air temperature increases. At the end of the trip, the rafts ride one more set of rapids, more like a series of small waves, before floating into a calm stretch of water. Lake Tugalo marks the end point of the river. A small motorboat waits to push the rafts, connected by carabineers, toward the takeout. Someone hands out cold beers. Upon reaching the destination, everyone helps the guides carry the big rubber crafts up to the waiting school bus, which ferries the exhausted, soggy, aching rafters back to warm, dry clothes. Their muscle soreness soon will fade, but their memories never will.

What a Tangled Web

A Lilliputian face, with six eyes, peeks out from a curled leaf. One leg grasps a telegraph line, waiting for the signal. The line twitches like a fishing rod. In a flash, something shoots out of the leaf and leaps on the victim, stickily entrapped. A marbled orbweaver has just captured a caddisfly, which has had the misfortune to bumble into her web. This little spider may be found in the Chattooga River watershed, making her living by spinning a web along the edge of a wood and waiting for lunch to be served. By day, she waits. By night, she retreats into her curled leaf, where she sometimes stores her food if she catches something but is not hungry. Her lair resembles a miniature meat locker, her prey wrapped and dangling by threads from the ceiling. The marbled orbweaver is a flamboyant spider that lives up to her name, being round and colorful. She begins bright yellow, but over time, her rotund abdomen blushes bright orange, making her look like a tiny pumpkin. In fact, an alternate name for her is the Halloween orbweaver. Her legs are bright red near the body and green with distal black bands that look like psychedelic socks.

Another interesting spider, one of about five hundred (of about forty thousand worldwide) that reside in the watershed, is the aptly named white-water fishing spider, which lives on the river and is about the size of a hand. You might expect this arachnid to be paddling a wee kayak; however, she is a diver. An eight-legged Jacques Cousteau, she encases herself in an air bubble, submerges and hunts underwater for insects and the occasional small fish. She also can walk on water, her delicate legs spaced widely apart as she tittups along the surface. You don't see these spiders frequently because they are very secretive, explains L.L. "Chick" Gaddy, a naturalist based in Columbia and Walhalla, South Carolina. They can live up to two years, during which time the male creeps onto the rock that the female calls home and tentatively mates with her. He leaves her with an egg sac, which she carries around in her jaws until finally fastening it to the rock. The young, called spiderlings, hatch in the spring and begin their own life cycle.

These spiders are big, says Gaddy, and "they will come after you." Once, a type of fishing spider somehow made it into his mountain cabin and was squatting on a bedside lampshade, perhaps trying to dry off. Gaddy, who is a pacifist concerning spiders, was ready to retire and "didn't want to sleep with a three-inch spider so close to my head" so decided to catch and release her. He cornered her, coat hanger for poking in one hand and towel for capturing in the other; the plan was to toss the towel over the spider and gently carry her outside, but she had other plans. "She didn't like it. She ran up the coat hanger at about one hundred miles per hour. Fortunately, I got my arm out of the way before she bit me," he recalls. He finally captured and released the spider in the woods, where she ran away.

A debate ensues over how painful a spider bite is compared to that of an insect. Fire ants are mentioned and then paper wasps, both of which inflict considerable agony. Bee stings aren't too bad, but yellow jacket stings, especially multiples, are intense. While yellow jackets and fire ants are aggressive, Gaddy points out, spiders "aren't sitting around waiting for you. But if you're in the wrong place at the wrong time, you could get bitten." He adds, hastily, "I wouldn't avoid the Chattooga River because of that." He's been bitten a couple of times by spiders. Once, he was "pinched and envenomed" on the nose by an orbweaver that fell into his glasses. A wolf spider somehow bit him on the lip, causing a tingling sensation but with no lasting effects. Most spiders are venomous but not dangerous to humans, at least not in this country. The only two (of more than seven hundred to one thousand) in the United States that have that distinction are the black widow, found in the Chattooga watershed; and the brown recluse, not found there. In contrast, visit Australia to encounter the funnel spider, one of the more than seventeen deadly arachnids to be found in the antipodes.

Gaddy, born in Timmonsville, South Carolina, is as stocky and solid as a fireplug. A Renaissance man, he has published several books, including *Spiders of the Carolinas* and *Biodiversity: Przewalski's Horse, Edna's Trillium, the Giant Squid, and Over 1.5 Million Other Species*, which he peppers with literary quotes from such luminaries as Ben Jonson, William Bartram, e.e. cummings, T.S. Eliot and Dylan Thomas. He is an environmental consultant for his own company, Terra Incognita, and is launching a book publishing company, Terra Incognita Books. He admits to having a photographic memory, explaining that it's almost a requirement for a naturalist. His memory banks, as he calls them, store the names of three hundred spiders, two thousand plants and four hundred birds (approximately). After finishing school, he worked for a short time for the South Carolina Department of Natural Resources but went off on his own in 1979. "I haven't had a real job since," he jokes.

Suddenly serious, he notes that the black widow, a deciduous woodland species, may be found in the Chattooga watershed. They lurk in the leaf litter by day, coming out at night to hunt. While they are poisonous, Gaddy explains, "the only way to get bitten is to put your finger in its web or walk barefoot through the woods at night," not advisable in any event. The black widow, of course, is black with a red hourglass-shaped tat on its abdomen and long, crooked legs—a classic horror-movie spider. Another watershed dweller is the spined Micrathena, a startling-looking representative of *Arachnida*, the spider class. With a spiny, camouflaged back, it resembles a diminutive armed tank. But, as with everything in nature, a purpose underlies this whimsical design. This three-quarter-inch spider is active during the day, when birds are hunting and would love nothing more than to consume this little protein packet. Her spines, however, make her hard to swallow and therefore safe from her winged predators. Therefore, this itsy-bitsy spider can be seen in the summer, lolling about in her web and waiting for hapless insects to blunder into her sticky trap—or for a hapless hiker to walk face first through her web, often strung across a trail opening (but known to the spider as an insect highway).

Possibly the most unusual spider found in the upper watershed is the Pocock lampshade spider, so called because of her web design. This three-inch specimen, with long, slender legs, is found in cool mountain gorges and spins her web on the under-hang of a rock. Narrower near the top than the bottom, the web looks like an upside-down splash, as well as a lampshade. The purpose of the dwelling is to provide a retreat as opposed to a trap; the spider runs around the surface of the rock to hunt for food. The male has extremely long legs so that he is able to reach into the web and court the female, which declines to come out for mating. If disturbed, she uses her web as a tiny trampoline, bouncing up and down in an effort to scare away the intruder.

Some people hate or fear spiders, but they won't bother you if you don't bother them. Like everything else in nature, they have a purpose and a right to exist, and like many other things in nature, their purpose incidentally benefits man. "If it weren't for spiders, we'd have more bugs," says Gaddy. In addition, webs have been used in traditional medicine to cover wounds and for blood clotting and are being looked at by science for these and other purposes. So consider the spider in her infinite variation next time you encounter her. Don't kill her. Innocent of malice, she toils and spins, waiting for her next meal and trying to avoid becoming someone else's.

Drop Me in the Water

Atruck inches up a long, curving road and stops. The driver looks furtively both ways before gunning right, heading down the mountain. Suddenly, a vehicle looms in his rearview mirror. He's being followed! He can't drive any faster or his barrels might hurtle out, spilling their precious contents all over the road. Moonshine? No, fish. The driver is transporting trout from the Walhalla State Fish Hatchery to be set free in the waters of the Chattooga River. On his tail is an eager angler who wants to see where the fish will be released. Then this cunning fisherman will throw in his line and try to outwit a wily trout—albeit hatchery raised and punch drunk after being scooped up, loaded into barrels, sloshed about during transit down winding mountain roads and thrown into a free-flowing river for the first time. "There used to be a faction of older gentlemen who would park at the hatchery, and when the trucks would leave, they would follow. It became a game between the drivers and the fishermen. We would run decoy trucks to mess with them," says Scott Poore, chuckling. Nowadays, however, the hatchery avoids stocking on set days in order to avoid being tailed. He and his staff must outwit the anglers, much as the anglers try to outwit the fish.

Poore manages the hatchery, located on Fish Hatchery Road in Mountain Rest, South Carolina, about twenty-one miles north of Walhalla off Highway 107. Tall and lean, sandy-haired and ruddy complexioned with a light goatee, he has worked there since 2007. He lives on the site, his house nestled in a sunny open area among the trees, overlooking the fish pens where the trout live. As you walk by the raceways, as they're called, the water lifts and falls like a blanket being shaken out. The trout have come to associate humans with food and are demanding their lunch.

The hatchery, built in the 1930s by the Civilian Conservation Corps, is one of five in South Carolina and the only facility that propagates coldwater fish. "The original fish hatcheries were designed to put back fish into rivers that had been damaged by logging, including the use of splash dams," explains Dan Rankin, regional fisheries coordinator of South Carolina's Department of Natural Resources (SC DNR). Splash dams were temporary barriers that constrained a river so that logs cut upstream would pile up behind them. When enough had accumulated, the dam was then blown up so that the logs would float downstream. Steel rods, the remains of one of these destructive methods of logging, can be seen under the waters of the West Fork of the Chattooga.

The hatchery, which released the first trout in 1937, was operated by the federal government until 1996. When budget cuts threatened to close the operation, the state took over management through the SC DNR. Poore explains that even though trout can reproduce in the Chattooga River, there's so much angling pressure that the population would be depleted if the hatchery did not support it. The hatchery's goal is to produce 470,000 fish per year; however, "the last five years have produced 750,000 to 900,000 or more trout into public waters." The hatchery stocks not only the Chattooga River but also the Chauga, the Eastatoe and parts of the Saluda, as well as Lake Jocassee. The trucks run once every seven to ten days from February through May and then September through about Thanksgiving. To reach the backcountry of the Chattooga, a helicopter is used for stocking.

The hatchery produces brown trout, rainbow trout and brook trout. Since the fish are in concrete pins, they don't reproduce naturally—maybe they're too modest to do it in public—so Poore and his four staff members assist. In October, the fish are ready to spawn, so first the biologists anesthetize them. Yes, anesthetize. They put the fish in special tanks and pour anesthesia over them. "They get very lethargic," Poore deadpans. The biologists then gently pick them up and "strip" the eggs, achieved by squeezing the fish with a downward motion along the abdomen, "kind of like milking a cow." The result looks like the filling for a sweet potato pie. Next, the males are relieved of their sperm, called milt, in the same manner. Not as much fun as the real thing, especially since they're unconscious, but more efficient. But how does one distinguish a male from a female fish? Actually, more easily than you might think: the jaws of a female are blunt and the males large and under-slung, sort of insouciant looking. Milt is added to the eggs,

The Walhalla Fish Hatchery under construction in the 1930s. *Photo courtesy of the South Carolina Department of Natural Resources.*

and the mixture is stirred, sort of like batter for a fish-egg cake. The eggs are incubated in an original hatchery building constructed, appropriately, with river rocks. On each of its double doors, a brass life-sized trout plaque hangs; to one side is another plaque reading, "Fish Propagated/Rainbow Trout/Brook Trout/Loch Leven Trout." (Loch Leven is another name for the brown trout and probably refers to the fish's point of origin.) Pride of workmanship emanates from these beautiful details. The interior smells fishy. Then again, it is a fish nursery.

Each female produces three thousand or more eggs, of which approximately 85 percent become fertilized. These future trout are incubated in an original hatchery building, in stacks of trays that hold about twenty-five thousand and provide constant oxygenation by means of a stream of fresh water drawn from the East Fork of the Chattooga, which runs adjacent to the hatchery. The biologists check the eggs daily, looking for black specks; these are the eyes, and these eggs are considered to be in the "eyed stage." As such, perhaps these fish-in-progress are able to observe events. In the next stage, they are transferred to a large cylindrical jar, where they bob about in circulating water. "What we're doing is mimicking exactly what's going on in the stream," Poore explains. The eggs gradually become fish. When the tiny trout reach about one-quarter of an inch long, they are called "fry," hinting of their future should they be caught by a hungry angler. At this point they are moved into a tank in the main room. They grow some more until they are considered "fingerlings," about the length of a finger, two to four inches long. The building contains ten tanks, all of which are filled with fifty to eighty thousand fry or fingerling. Fry, new to the world, swim aimlessly about the tank if you lean over it to look at them. However, the fingerlings have figured out that people equal food and follow any warm body from one side of their tank to the other. They crave a fishy-smelling meal of menhaden, which is derived from another type of fish. Poore dips a net into a tank and scoops out a few fingerlings, what Angler Barbie might catch with her petite fly rod. They squirm vigorously, perhaps envisioning future struggles with a fisherman, until Poore tips them gently back into the water.

Although they don't realize it, these trifling trout are waiting to graduate to the raceways outside. When the time comes, they are moved into one-hundred-foot-long concrete enclosures, each of which holds about twelve to fifteen thousand trout. Each of the twenty-four raceways holds a separate species, grouped by age. When they reach between nine and twelve inches, about a year after hatching, they're released into the wild. By this time, they seem almost tame. Begging for food, they follow anyone who walks by their pen. The water shivers and seethes. "They seem to get domesticated," observes Poore, but he adds that they never truly lose their wildness. While initially these newbies are easy pickings for an angler, "it doesn't take long for those fish to learn that the same bait's being thrown in, and they're being caught out." Once they figure it out, "they tend to lock down and then you've got to change your presentation." Now it's becoming clear why those men wanted to wet their lines as soon as the fish were stocked; the trout have not yet lost their innocence, so to speak. Not very sporting, it seems, but not everyone plays fair. At least the trout feel at home when they are released, as all the water in their tanks is captured from the river and cycled back out again. The hatchery complies with the Clean Water Act and submits to inspections by the Department of Health and Environmental Control.

One raceway contains what might be called retired fish, Methuselahs of troutdom, up to four feet long and weighing ten pounds or more. Languidly, they drift through the water, looking prehistoric and unconcerned. One is gaping his mouth open in an absurd manner, and Poore leans over, eyebrows lifting, to get a closer look. "I don't know why he's doing that," he remarks. While these senior trout have lost their youthful vigor, a trout in its prime is streamlined perfection. Rainbows look like a bit of currency or a piece of the river, silvery with a stripe of pink on their bellies. Brookies have what looks like confetti thrown on their sides: red dots encircled by blue against greenish-brown and a swipe of orange. Browns are much more festive than their name suggests, sporting green backs and a smattering of red and black polka dots finished with a yellow belly.

Trout can live up to thirty years, but the stocked ones survive perhaps seven years if they don't get caught by anglers or other predators. The taste for trout flesh also is strong in otters, raccoons, kingfishers and great blue herons; Poore points to a gap in the chain-link fence surrounding the raceways, indicating where these hungry fish hunters sneak in. They can't be blamed; trout is mild and delicious, probably the least fishy-tasting of all fish. Since they have reduced scales, they are easy to prep for cooking: just pull out the entrails and they're ready to fry, broil or bake. If you've caught many creels full of trout and cooked them over a campfire or at home (sautéed with lemon and stuffed with garlic), it's hard to order them off a menu; the best chef can't capture the taste of a fresh trout caught and cooked by yourself. Poore agrees. After working with trout all day, he doesn't have any desire to fish them out of the stream in which he just put them. In fact, maybe blasphemously, he prefers bass fishing.

In addition to being a fish factory, so to speak, the hatchery also is a learning center. Poore leads tours of schoolchildren and other interested groups, explaining that the hatchery is a popular tourist destination. "I manage people as much as I manage fish," he jokes, and he clearly enjoys that aspect of his job. Good thing, as sixty to seventy tours and fifty to sixty thousand people per year visit the hatchery. Beside the hatchery office is a refitted gumball machine, offering ground menhaden for twenty-five cents. Apparently, people will pay to feed fishmeal to other fish, perpetuating a sort of piscine cannibalism.

While the hatchery is located in Sumter National Forest, it is on state land and is managed by SC DNR. The hatchery does not receive state-appropriated funds, depending instead on sportfish restoration money. Tackle, bait, boat gas, rods and so on support the operation, which also receives financial aid from Duke Power and the Army Corps of Engineers for what is called mitigation funds: the two entities dammed streams to produce power and recreational opportunities, in the forms of Lakes Jocassee and Hartwell, and as such pay for the loss of free-flowing water. This independence from state-allocated money keeps the hatchery from the budget chopping block because the influx of income stays fairly constant. People keep fishing regardless of what the economy's doing, possibly more so in bad times. Fishing has a soothing, almost sedative effect that diminishes everything but the fishing rod, the flow of water and the delicious tension of waiting for a trout to take the hook.

Stocking ensures that whenever an angler throws a cast, he or she will most likely catch something. This bet is hedged during what's called delayed harvest: during early November through early May, anglers must release any fish they catch. "Anglers want to be assured of catching fish when they come from far away, such as Columbia or even Charleston," says Poore. Starting in May, the fish in these locations can be harvested because they most likely won't live through the summer, succumbing in high temperatures. The Chattooga represents the southernmost range of the trout, a species that requires cold water.

Why do people go to such lengths to fish? Why fertilize fish by hand, drop them by helicopter into a river, stand in cold water hour after hour waiting for one to bite, only to release it? Sometimes in life, there are no answers. If you like to fish, no explanation is necessary; if you don't, no explanation is possible.

The Life of a Caddisfly

Beneath the surface of the river, something wormlike, but segmented, darts through the water and disappears into a crack in a stone. Slowly, a head peers out and two sharp mandibles click together. Sensing that the coast is clear, the creature crawls out onto the surface of the rock. It's about a half inch long, bright green and mottled with brown; it looks like a bit of algae, the better to fool predator and prey. Three legs on each side of its upper body sport tiny claws, which enable it to more securely clasp the rock face. What looks like a pair of grappling hooks projects from its posterior end. The creature looks like the star of a science-fiction horror movie, something that would crawl into a person's ear and wreak havoc. But this miniature monster is actually a caddisfly larva, not dangerous to anything but organic matter and perhaps other insect larvae. While not many people may know a caddisfly from a Cadbury crème egg, this insect has a very important role in the life of a river.

The adult caddisfly is a delicate thing, with four lacey, membranous wings and a slender body that can range in color from silver to orange. They also brandish two whip-like antennae, sometimes twice as long as their bodies. Ecologically, they are related to mayflies—described lyrically as "lifelong dancers of a day" by poet Richard Wilbur—and like mayflies, they aren't designed to do much but reproduce. In fact, mayflies don't even have functional mouths. They hatch, emerging from the water by the millions; conduct a magnificent aerial display as they search frantically for mates; copulate, lay eggs and die, sometimes all on the same day. The adult caddisfly can eat but, because of its "sponging mouthparts," sups lightly on nectar or perhaps a little aphid honeydew, says John Morse, an entomologist at Clemson University. Morse most likely is the world's leading authority on the caddisfly and manages the Trichoptera World Checklist. In 1969, he completed his master's thesis, an inventory of caddisflies in the mountains of South Carolina; he collected at ten sites every night for a year while attending classes during the day. His findings doubled the number of species identified in the state.

Every known organism is identified using taxonomy, or the scientific system of classification, which was developed by Carl Linnaeus in 1758 to provide consistency for all animals so that scientists would know precisely what species was being referred to when someone said, for instance, *Rhyacophila carolina*. This designation translates to "Carolina stream lover" and is a species of caddisfly common to the Chattooga. Each species is organized into the following classifications: kingdom, phylum, class, order, family, genus and species. The Carolina stream lover is classified thus: Kingdom Animalia, Phylum Arthropoda, Class Hexapoda, Order Trichoptera, Family Rhyacophilidae, Genus *Rhyacophila* and species *R. carolina*. Linnaeus chose a dead language (Latin, or Latinized Greek) to name living things because it was universal and not likely to evolve, being dead. Caddisflies fall into Tricoptera, the seventh-largest order of insects. Approximately 15,000 caddisfly species are known worldwide; the Chattooga River is home to about 150 species, according to Morse. He says up to 1,000 other aquatic insect species also may be found in the Chattooga.

The importance of a universal classification system is illuminated when you realize how many species of insects exist on Earth: estimates range as high as 80 million, according to Dr. Terry Erwin of the Smithsonian Institute. According to Robert G. Foottit and Peter H. Adler, in their 2009 book *Insect Biodiversity: Science and Society*, 1,004,898 species of insects exist, representing about two-thirds (58 to 67 percent) of all plant and animal species; possibly 10 quintillion (a 10 followed by *seventeen more* zeros) individual insects are alive at a given time.

Like every other organism on Earth, the ultimate purpose of the caddisfly is to reproduce. The beginning, for a caddisfly, is an egg, which is encased with hundreds of others in "a sticky matrix, a sort of jelly ball," Morse describes. Laid close to or in water, the eggs hatch in a couple of weeks; the resulting larvae enter their new aquatic environment. Here they make a living, fossicking around in the streambed searching for food, including tiny bits of organic matter resting on the bottom of the stream, as well as algae, fungi, plant material and other organisms, says Morse. Some even weave "little fishing nets they build in the water and use to catch food." In addition, the larvae act as a sort of aquatic earthworm, chewing up dead sticks and leaves, breaking them down and then depositing them via their excrement. As Morse puts it, "They are crucial in the transformation of organic nutrients from tiny particles into larger ones and of larger ones to smaller ones." Caddisfly larvae not only eat but also are eaten, by fish, other insects, spiders, crawfish, birds, bats and other animals in the food chain.

Caddisflies have other interesting habits. Some species of caddisfly larvae move freely in a stream, where they hide in cracks and chase insect prey. However, others creatively "build a little house they carry around, built of bits of sticks, sand and even the houses of other species of caddisfly larvae" containing the occupant, which then gets a piggyback ride. "They look like a little Medusa," Morse chuckles. This ingenious adaptation provides physical protection and camouflage for the soft-bodied larva. In addition, they use these "little tubes" to assist respiration by drawing in a fresh supply of oxygenated water and pushing it out with rhythmic undulations of the body.

Some of these architecturally inclined caddisfly larvae fashion their little houses out of mussel shells or pebbles; Morse once saw one that had precisely and symmetrically applied tiny twigs of gradually shortening lengths, on four sides, from top to bottom. The result, a gradually narrowing tube of stacked squares, looked like a miniature art-deco statue. When you see something this elegant and orderly, you may be tempted to suspect that these insects actually think about and plan their designs. However, their behavior is "hardwired by genetics, including a range of possible adaptations of that behavior according to different environmental conditions," explains Morse. Basically, they use whatever's available to them but sometimes with stunning results that rival any artist's. In fact, jewelry maker Kathy Kyle considers the designs to be little masterpieces. She collects and raises caddisfly larvae, offering them materials not readily available on the bottom of a stream. Using opals, amethysts, turquoise, gold and other precious gems and minerals, these artisans construct works of art. Kyle then removes each larva from its tube and returns it to the stream from which it was collected, using the empty vessel to create a one-of-a-kind piece of jewelry. Presumably, the evicted larvae either rebuild or transition into adults.

Left to their devices, the larvae grow all year, capturing food to nourish their growing bodies. They pass through five "instars," a poetic description of the developmental stage, in which they change subtly as they progress

An adult caddisfly, delicate wings folded, rests on a log. *Photo by Thomas Ames.*

toward adulthood. If they avoid becoming someone else's meal, the larvae finally enter the pupal stage, where they dwell for about two or three weeks. When they emerge as adults, they couldn't look more different from their aquatic selves—from sci-fi monsters to winged ephemera. After a brief spell on the earth, they flutter off on their last adventure: to find a mate. After copulating, they alight on the water or dive beneath it, perch on a rock alongside the river or dangle from an overhanging tree branch or bridge abutment. Their last act is to lay eggs, the promise of the next generation. The wheel of life turns once more.

The caddisfly's importance to the river cannot be overstated. If for some reason all of them disappeared, the river would die. "It would be a disaster," says Morse, a lean sixty-something wearing a crew cut and glasses with thick black frames. "The food chain would break down completely. The fish would die. It would stink," and the same cause would also kill stoneflies, mayflies and other aquatic species. However, a total caddisfly wipeout would never happen, Morse assures, because "different species are differentially sensitive to pollution and different kinds of pollution." This realization has led to an elegant method of testing the health of a river using insects, and the unassuming caddisfly is an indicator species, as well as part of the food chain. Morse explains that caddisflies and other insects are scaled for tolerance from zero to ten, with zero equaling absolute aversion for a pollutant. A community is sampled and the species identified; if the sample contains a lot of species that possess zero tolerance for pollution, then the water is deemed pristine.

According to this criterion, says Morse, the Chattooga River, which has a high density and diversity of caddisflies, is "in pretty good shape, especially near the headwaters." The most common pollutant Morse has seen on the Chattooga is sediment. Sediments issue from roadwork, road crossings over the river or "any kind of activity that removes vegetation and causes erosion." What sediment does is fill the cracks and crevices in and among the rocks on the streambed, where insects like to hide to avoid fish. "They have no place to live; the sediment becomes a pollutant that destroys their habitat," he says.

Currently, standard water-quality protocols exist in every state, and insects are used for "ambient monitoring," the testing of a general area as opposed to a specific site, say downstream of a sewage treatment plant. These tests give a good overall indication of water quality. James Glover, manager of the Aquatic Section of the Bureau of Water at South Carolina's Department of Health and Environmental Control (SC DHEC), describes the process, known as bio-assessment, and expands on Morse's explanation: "We use an index called EPT, which stands for the three orders of insects that are very tolerant to pollution." The orders include mayflies, stoneflies and caddisflies (with Latin names **E**phemeroptera, **P**lecoptera and **T**richoptera, respectively). These insects offer a twenty-four-hour, daily monitoring system that is more effective than simply sampling water, explains Glover. Insects stay put, while water flows, taking pollutants with it. In other words, insects, being stationary, demonstrate exposure to a pollutant after the effected water has washed downstream. As Morse puts it, "They also respond to the combined effects of all potentially important pollutants in a way that is impossible to measure in a chemical laboratory."

The Chattooga River has an EPT index of sixty to sixty-five, says Glover, meaning that sixty to sixty-five individual species of "bio-indicators" (mayflies, stoneflies and caddisflies) are found in a water sample. His agency samples eight hundred sites, representing thousands of miles of streams, and the Chattooga River, heavily forested without much human encroachment, is the cleanest. A direct correlation exists between urbanization and pollution, as you would expect, and the Chattooga is relatively free of either. His agency has one collection site, on Highway 76, which is sampled every other month. The mission of SC DHEC is to carry out the mandate of the Clean Water Act of 1972, which requires the agency to "maintain and restore the physical, chemical and biological integrity of the waters of the nation," says Glover. The Environmental Protection Agency, created in 1970, holds ultimate authority, but each state partners with this entity, and each other when necessary, to ensure that the laws are enforced. Little do most people know that the humble caddisfly plays an important role in this process. Who would guess that with all the high technology available, an insect is the go-to for water pollution?

Seeing Beyond Your Own Bait

When you go fishing, whether you're alone or with friends, you're by yourself," says Art Shick. If this statement seems to contradict itself, you aren't a fisherman. If you were, you'd know that when you cast, the world goes away. "It's solitary. Just you and your thoughts," he says. He remembers the first time he laid eyes on the Chattooga River, one afternoon in late July. "The sun was hitting the water just right, so that all the mica crystals were dancing. I thought, 'This is it.'" Not long after, "It" happened: Shick moved his family from Ohio to Walhalla in 1987. What drew him was the Chattooga.

What began as a selfish act ended in an unselfish one; Shick's move to the South initially was for his own benefit, yet he ended up doing more than wetting his line. He is one of those people who can see beyond the bait on his hook, so to speak. He knew that in order to sustain the fish, the river must be protected. While fishing "has to have an element of selfishness, there's a point where you have to put more emphasis on the 'we' as opposed to the 'I,'" he explains. Fishermen often speak poetically without trying. And fishing, also known as angling, is full of contradictions, such as the act of "catch and release." You catch a fish; then you put it back in the river. Why bother? If you aren't an angler, you won't understand.

In 1988, he and three friends started the Chattooga River Chapter of Trout Unlimited (TU). The closest charter until that time was in Greenville, and Shick and his friends believed that Oconee County could support a chapter closer to the Chattooga. In addition, they recognized the need for a local chapter of an organization designed to protect the local resources. After all, you can't swing a catfish without hitting a stream in the mountains of South Carolina. They were right: the chapter started with about forty-five members and has grown to about two hundred. "The orientation is primarily the protection of the resource by a bunch of fishermen. Getting together to talk fish stories did not make a club," Shick relates, summoning the vision of a roomful of anglers, arms stretched wide to demonstrate the length of their last catch. Shick served on the board, including as its first president, for twenty years before recently stepping down, citing his age as the reason. While he claims to be seventy, he looks twenty years younger: lean and fit, face free of lines, steel gray hair and goatee shot with black. Perhaps his youthfulness is a benefit of fishing.

The Chattooga chapter's first project was the restoration of Corbin Creek, which was supported with funding from the national office of TU and Duke Power. Members removed beaver dams, which heat up the water, reduce the oxygen content and contribute to the buildup of silt—all detrimental to trout, which need cold, clear, fast-moving, oxygenated water to survive. Currently, the chapter partners with the South Carolina Department of Natural Resources (SC DNR) in an effort to restore the brook trout, the only trout native to this region, to several small streams including tributaries of the Chattooga. The brookie, the most sensitive of the trout, was extirpated from the Chattooga watershed in the early 1900s; deforestation by loggers resulted in increased temperature and siltation, which doomed the species. However, the trees have since reestablished themselves along the streams, shading them and making them once again amenable habitat for the brookie.

The first step of the restoration process is to eliminate any nonnative species of trout that may be living in the targeted streams. "Brookies are the smallest of trout," explains David Van Lear, who has been a member of TU for more than fifty years and assisted in the restoration effort. A retired forestry professor at Clemson University, Van Lear is gray-haired and soft spoken, wearing a sweet expression and glasses; he's the kind of teacher students love. He continues: "We removed all the other species of trout from isolated streams barred by impassable obstacles" in the chosen tributaries so that they would not be able to swim back up from the river. Then they replaced them with brook trout. Why go to all the trouble when the restored streams aren't going to be fished? Van Lear cites conservation ethics, defined as "the maintenance and restoration of population viability and ecosystem health" by the Conservation Ethics Group. "We wouldn't want a species to go extinct in a stream we were charged to manage," he says, adding that it would reflect badly on his generation of anglers if they let the brookie go "because it didn't count much for my fishing experience." Brookies are small, about four to six inches long, and not exactly an adrenaline rush to land. However, says Van Lear, "They are gorgeous. They look like aquarium fish," with their speckles and splashes of color. Dan Rankin, regional fisheries coordinator of the SC DNR, agrees: "It's a no-brainer because the brook trout is ingrained in our heritage. Plus, it's such a pretty fish."

Brook trout are special to Art Shick, too. He recalls the first one he caught, up North, during the era of polluted streams with water as opaque as chocolate milk. "It was a knockout sensation to see that fish," he says. It's easy to understand why he was enchanted by a brookie, which looks like a party favor. These festively colored fish will reproduce in the restored streams but will not live in the Chattooga itself. The water temperature is too high, made warmer over the years by past logging operations, tree die-off and climate change. Even if the water were cold enough for the brookie, it would be out-competed by the stocked rainbow and brown trout, which are more tolerant of warmer water. "At this point, the Chattooga can only be a managed river," says Shick, meaning that rainbows and browns will have to be stocked in order for fishing to continue as a concern.

While Shick admits it's more exciting to "fish over wild trout" than the stocked version, he says the Chattooga is his favorite river. Many people feel this way about it, but no one has a clear answer, and no one's reason is the same. Trying to capture the reason is akin to trying to follow the same drop of water from the top of Whiteside Mountain down the Chattooga and into Lake Tugalo. However, Shick explains that it does have something to do with the fact that the river "is in the forest from the beginning." Like most serious fishermen, he uses a fly rod 99 percent of the time. "I have been known to use bait. But," he adds tactfully, "only for catfish." Fly fishers often view bait fishers as the abecedarians of angling, and certainly no one ever waxes mystic about a rod and reel. Shick tries to explain why fly-fishing inspires such a spiritual state: "You have a change. You slow down, have a restfulness." Such feelings seem ineffable, as hard to capture as a dragonfly on the wing.

Not all fishing experiences involve fish, as most fishermen know. Shick is no different. He was fishing near Burrell's Ford and decided to take a break, so he settled himself on a rock to sit and smoke a pipe. Then he noticed the dragonfly larvae. "They were about to break out. They were coming out, unfolding their wings. It was amazing, a major memory," he relates. He watched for the hour it took for the insects to complete their metamorphosis.

He's also seen otters, beavers and rattlesnakes, and once a young deer walked past him so closely, he says, "I could've brushed it with my hand."

In a world in which immediate gratification isn't soon enough, people like Art Shick and David Van Lear demonstrate the beauty and satisfaction of waiting: for a fish to bite, for a species to be restored, for a dragonfly to unfurl its wings for the first time. In number, through groups like Trout Unlimited, they model the act of letting go of the "I" to embrace the "we." From the love of fishing springs the love of fish, motivating people like them to restore the long-missing brook trout to its historic home. Instead of saying, "I want it all, and I want it now," these men say, "Here is this gift, for the sake of giving, for the future."

A Pair of Ragged Claws

Under a rock lurks a tiny monster, eyes on stalks, antenna waving, claws questing. Startled by a pair of probing paws, it shoots backward to escape capture from a hungry raccoon. Once safe, the crayfish resumes its own search for food. Although resembling a mini lobster, this little decapod is more creative when it comes to color. This particular species is the white tubercled crayfish, one of several that can be found in the Chattooga River. The white tubercled crayfish has a golden-beige head and body and a delicate sprinkling of black and white dots with a flourish of red across its back. Each segment of the abdomen—its posterior tail-like appendage—sports epaulets of black stripes and red dots. However, the creature's proudest possession, should it happen to be vain, has to be its claws. They look like a magnificent pair of black gloves such as a swordsman would don, decorated with little white bumps called tubercles. The joints are red, coordinating perfectly with the crayfish's cape and epaulets.

The crayfish is, in fact, related to the lobster, as well as to crabs and shrimps. In scientific speak, their phylum is Arthropoda, meaning they have jointed legs; class Crustacea, meaning they possess hard shells; order Decapoda, referring to their ten legs. Of the more than 550 species live worldwide, 400 reside in North America, "the Southeastern United States being the center of global diversity," according to "Crayfishes of Georgia" on the Georgia College website. Georgia is home to about 70 species of crayfish, 17 of which are found nowhere else in the world. About a half-dozen are found in the waters of the Chattooga River, whether in North Carolina, South Carolina or Georgia. Crayfish don't respect state boundaries.

Christopher Skelton is a biology professor at Georgia College, located in Milledgeville. He specializes in crayfish, which also are known as crawfish. Formerly a zoologist for the Georgia Department of Natural Resources, he recalls how he got started on this path: "While collecting for fish, we used to pull up a lot of crayfish. I would wonder what kind they were, but no one knew." Later, he conducted a study of the creature, which solidified his interest and made him the crackerjack crayfish guy in Georgia. He even identified a species new to science. He runs the "Crayfishes of Georgia" website, an extremely well-organized catalogue of its subject. The main page features a close-up of a stunning, indigo-blue specimen, followed by a description of the website and an introduction to the crayfishes of the state. On the left is a key that will guide the user to a list of Georgia species, a species list by drainage and a map depicting crayfish ranges, as well as a description of how to identify crayfish, crayfish ecology and life history, a glossary and links to other sources.

The types of crayfish that you might find in the Chattooga watershed include the common crayfish, the variable crayfish, the disjunct crayfish and the delightfully named mitten crayfish. The mitten crayfish, which most likely would be found hiding under a rock in a Chattooga River tributary, has the same orangey-red carapace as its cousin the lobster. The name refers to its impressive claws, which are not only huge but also hairy. Whatever the species, the crayfish uses its claws to capture food: leaf litter, dead organic matter, "each other, whatever they can get their hands [claws?] on or overpower," according to Skelton in a telephone interview. In turn, they are eaten by whatever can get hands, or fins, on them: fish, raccoons, minks, whatever is prepared to look under river rocks to find them. In short, "Crayfish eat everything, and everything eats crayfish," an old crayfish truism. But crayfish have a couple of tricks up their...claws. First, the claws themselves: "They will always try to pinch you," says Skelton. The second is their ability to shoot backward very fast, a maneuver the scientists have designated "tail flipping."

Most of the species described on the Georgia Crayfish website are accompanied by beautiful, glossy, centerfoldish photographs of the crayfish posing in their habitats or facsimiles of such. Skelton explains how he happened to have such exquisite representations: one day, his phone rang, and a heavily accented German voice informed him that the caller would like to come to Georgia to photograph crayfish. The photographer, Chris

Lukhaup, who also is a member of a death-metal band, shot many of the crayfish featured on the website. Among them is the devil crawfish, olive-green edged with flame, looking like Lucifer's slightly ridiculous sidekick; the Piedmont blue burrower, a gorgeous metallic-blue specimen, shimmering like a disco ball; the longnose, which is the color of a perfectly ripe, unblemished banana; and the greensaddle, so dazzling that words cannot do it justice. One is whimsically called the Christmas tree crayfish, decked with the greens and reds of the yuletide. One never knew how many species of crayfish exist, or how beautiful and varied they are, representing all the colors of a crustacean rainbow. Someone had fun naming them, too: the ambiguous crayfish, for example. Can't he make up his mind? The mountain midget, the ditch-fencing crayfish, the poor crayfish and the sly crayfish all scuttle through life, heedless of their amusing names. The Vidalia crayfish seems

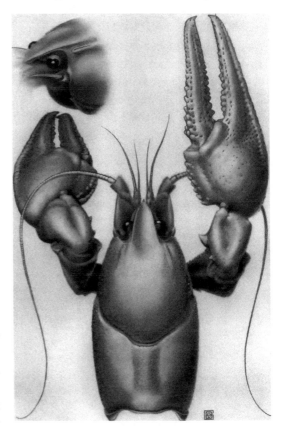

like it should be waving an onion. Whoever named the ornate crayfish must have been mocking it, because it's a dull reddish-brown—not very sexy compared to some of its cousins. If you like Cajun food, your mouth will start watering if you look at the photo of the red swamp crawfish, sometimes ignominiously referred to as a "mudbug." Skelton says that while you can eat any crayfish, the mudbug is conducive to growing for food and is bigger and, therefore, more cost effective. Whatever its name, it's delicious.

The life cycle of an aquatic crayfish is more complicated than you might imagine. The males only can mate when they're dressed in courting clothes

Anatomy of a crawfish. *Taken from a 1981 report,* The Crawfishes of Georgia, *by Horton H. Hobbs Jr.*

or, in scientific terms, in "first form condition." Only in this stage can they pass sperm, says Skelton. Otherwise, they are more casually attired, in "second form condition." They mate in the fall or spring, molting back and forth between forms as needed, probably because it costs too much energy to maintain their mating duds. When appropriately accoutered, the male presents a female with a "sperm plug," which she carries until she's ready to lay eggs, sometimes months later. Once she decides to move forward with the process, she attaches the eggs, by "little feathery things" called swimmerets, to her abdomen. She now is considered "in berry," because the little egg packet resembles a cluster of berries. Crayfish biologists have a wonderful sense of humor. Endearingly, when the baby crayfishlets (not the scientific term) hatch, they remain tethered to their mother by threads. In this state, they grow and molt a couple of times, then let go and drift away to start their own life journeys. They live approximately two to three years, Skelton says, but some cave species, which are another story, are thought to live for decades.

Currently, none of the crayfish in the Chattooga watershed is endangered. However, Skelton warns that this state could change. The biggest threat, to this and most other species of plants or animals, is habitat destruction, but a close second is the introduction of an invasive species of crayfish that could out-compete the natives. Such a scenario is possible, as when anglers using crayfish for bait release the leftovers, or if one escapes—or if a child lets one go after a school project because he or she didn't want to kill it. A favorite parental adage, "Put things back where they belong," may be re-imagined when dealing with living things: "*Don't* put things where they *don't* belong."

Take a Hike

That is *probably* edible," says Greg Lucas of what looks like an orange ping-pong paddle stuck to the side of a dying hemlock. The growths are bracket fungi and are, in fact, safe to eat. However, Lucas's qualifier is the best approach to fungi or mushrooms; if any doubt exists, assume they may be poisonous. Lucas, a biologist for the SC DNR, and his daughter Caroline join a small group of others on a muggy, overcast, late spring day for a hike to a waterfall on King Creek, a tributary of the Chattooga River. Hike leader Richard Cain sets a comfortable pace, stopping to point out interesting plants, such as the Indian cucumber root. "That *is* edible," he assures. The hikers, members of the Foothills Trail Conference, meander through the woods and down a path into a gorge, through which flows King Creek. "I don't believe in the supernatural, but I think ticks just materialize," Cain declares after Lucas discovers one scuttling across his hand. Cain, who is a retired teacher and amateur naturalist, is a fit sixty-four-year-old with an engaging demeanor, a ZZ Top beard and a ladybug earring. As the hikers amble along, he relates stories of his former employment. He once paddled his kayak in a dark, water-filled cave looking for bats, an experience he says he would not like to repeat. "My brain stem was twitching," he shudders. The group stops as Lucas points out an American chestnut sapling. This tree once was the dominant species in the Appalachian Mountains until it was decimated by a malignant foreign fungus, the infamous chestnut blight. In a warped turn of fate, the sapling will live a few years, yearning toward the sun, before succumbing to the blight.

As the path turns upstream, the conversation turns to skunks. "Anyone else think they *don't* smell bad?" poses Cain. The sound of falling water grows louder as the hikers debate the odoriferosity of the little striped mammal. Someone points out that they are related to minks, the scent glands of which are used as a base for perfume. After a one-mile hike, the explorers reach the base of King Creek Falls, an impressive cascade that plunges seventy feet, releasing a fine mist of water that nourishes the surrounding verdant surfaces. The high rocks cupping the falls host spray cliff communities, specialized collections of plants that live only in this type of environment. They look like miniature rain forests where fairies might abide. Liverwort, walking fern, mountain wood sorrel, sphagnum and other species of plants quiver and glisten in the moist breeze billowing off the waterfall. On the damp underside of a rock, a lampshade spider lurks, waiting for an insect to blunder into its clutches. Lucas informs the group that King Creek is one of the tributaries being stocked with brook trout. They're being placed above the falls so that they will not be able to swim downstream into the river, where they would have to compete with stocked rainbows and browns. After photos are snapped, the hikers start back.

Most days in the Chattooga River corridor are sunny and mild, ideal for year-round hiking. Spring offers the experience of rebirth, as trees shoot out tender green buds and birds compete vociferously for mates and territory. In the sweltering temperatures of summer, the river offers a refreshing respite and makes a hot hike worth the effort and sweat. Fall bittersweetly demonstrates that death can be beautiful, as leaves turn from green to red, yellow and orange before letting go to join generations of their brethren in the mulch. Winter is a curtain parted to reveal stunning views of the Blue Ridge Escarpment, cascading waterfalls and outcroppings of giant rocks that have hurled themselves from the mountainsides to rest among the trees and in the river. Winter hiking also offers respite from summer's biting insects, as well as snakes, which hibernate during the cold months.

Something about being in the woods is restorative. Add to that the sound of water, which both soothes and energizes, for an ideal combination. The Chattooga River Trail, the Bartram Trail and the Foothills Trail share a course along the Chattooga before diverging in separate directions, offering the day hiker, the angler or the backpacker solitude, exercise and beautiful scenery. The trails wind through scenic and diverse landscapes abounding with flora and fauna: deep mountain hollows rarely visited by the sun; ridges offering panoramic views of the Blue Ridge Mountains; sun-flecked glens that look like they harbor hobbits; rushing streams that cascade over rocks and transform into waterfalls; and bears, deer, turkey, hawks, eagles, woodpeckers and a plethora of other wildlife. Turtles trundle, snakes slide. While the copperhead and the timber rattler are found in the watershed, these are the only two venomous snakes found there. Many species of plants proliferate, including a variety of orchid called Jack-in-the pulpit; the delicate filmy fern with its nearly transparent leaves; and the rare Oconee bell hiding in cool, damp gorges.

The Chattooga River Trail runs 37.7 miles, starting at the South Carolina/North Carolina border near Ellicott Rock Wilderness Area, which includes 3.5 miles of the trail. Running 17.3 miles through South Carolina downstream to the SC Highway 28 Bridge, the Chattooga River Trail then meanders 20.0 miles through Georgia before ending close to Clayton. Rated moderate, the trail winds though the forest over high bluffs and crosses numerous streams. The stretch close to Licklog Creek hugs the river's edge and provides access to swimming holes, sandy strips, good angling opportunities and numerous waterfalls, including King Creek, Spoonauger, Big Bend, Pig Pen and Licklog Falls. While the trail does not afford views of the rapids, the roar of Bull Sluice can be heard as the hiker approaches the end of the trail. The Bartram Trail, named for eighteenth-century explorer and botanist William Bartram, runs 37.0 miles, 10.0 of which merge with the Chattooga River Trail. The Foothills Trail, 77.0 miles long, shares 8.5 miles with the other two and was listed as "one of the best long trails (50+ miles) in the country" by *Backpacker Magazine* in 2011.

Risk is inherent in any outdoor activity, so the would-be hiker should be prepared. The Forest Service Ranger Station, located on Highway 28 about ten miles northwest of Walhalla en route to the river, offers maps and other materials, including the rules concerning camping and boating. Even though the Chattooga is considered pristine, toting water is a must, especially in hot weather. When the weather

Morning sun lights the river. *Photo by Peter McIntosh.*

starts to cool, layers are appropriate, as the temperature can drop quickly. Darkness also falls quickly in the mountains, so explorers should keep up with the time and let someone know where they're going and approximately when they'll return. Cellphones don't work reliably in the deep gorges, but a personal global positioning system (GPS) can alert emergency personnel in case of accident. The Department of Natural Resources provides schedules for hunting season, which is allowed in parts of the corridor, and anyone who enters the woods during these times is urged to wear bright clothing. Hikers are advised to stay on marked trails to avoid getting lost in the thousands of acres that blanket the area and not to climb on the rocks or wade and swim above waterfalls, rapids, fast-moving or high water. Other useful items to carry are first-aid and snakebite kits; field guides for plant, tree, bird and animal identification; and, most of all, a sense of wonder.

Of Microclimates and Men

Trilliums are more diverse per square inch in the Southern Blue Ridge Escarpment than anywhere else on the planet, according to Patrick McMillan. In fact, he says, more species exist in a single cove than can be found in any other state. This enchanting wildflower, with its signature three leaves, is fairly restricted to a small area and at the mercy of the climate. It might not exist at all if not for a very special quality of the region. The story begins with ants, which disperse the seeds of the trillium. Since ants can't travel very fast, neither do the seeds. They don't travel far either—perhaps only one hundred feet—to produce the next generation of trillium, and it takes seven to ten years for the plant to reach adulthood and form the next seed. The tale continues with climate change. "To really survive, you have to be able to move," McMillan says, referring to the fact that species tend to migrate: to warmer regions when the climate cools, as in an ice age; or to cooler climes when it warms. Yet even though the trillium cannot move fast or far, it somehow has survived perhaps millions of years, including through the ages of glacial cold. Something happened that allowed this species, a dispersal-limited plant found nowhere else on earth, to survive in the Southern Blue Ridge Escarpment, says McMillan: "You have to assume that place provided a sheltering resiliency during the upheaval of climate change."

The region also has the highest diversity of salamanders per square inch found anywhere, which further demonstrates the resiliency of the place. As McMillan says, "Salamanders can't walk away" when the climate gets cold. "They are at the mercy of climate change," yet they, too, survived ice ages. How?

The answer is microclimates, which are pockets—coves, drainages, gorges—in which conditions stay relatively stable even in the face of global climate changes. "The Blue Ridge Escarpment is resilient because of these microclimates," says McMillan. Many salamander species living in the Chattooga River corridor are lungless, breathing through their skins; they must remain wet or they will die. One of the resident salamanders has the distinction of possessing lungs and being the South Carolina state amphibian. Resembling a scrap of confetti, the spotted salamander hides in and around water.

More evidence for the microclimate phenomenon is found in the distribution of the Oconee bell, a modest white wildflower found entirely in the Blue Ridge Escarpment eco-region, even though "it probably grows better in Michigan than in South Carolina because it has a high tolerance to cold." Why, then, doesn't it grow in Michigan? Like the trillium, the Oconee bell is not good at reproducing; its seeds, unassisted by ants, have a hard time germinating and traveling. Interestingly, the Oconee bell has relatives in China, Taiwan and Japan. These species of the plant probably developed millions of years ago across a band of similar climate across the globe, becoming restricted when climates changed, fragmented by the movement of ice through the ages. The conditions in these regions, however, remained similar, which is why similar species are found in these far-apart places. In a manner of speaking, they exist in parallel universes.

Born in Florida and raised in the mountains of North Carolina, McMillan is a member of that vanishing species, the naturalist. His grandmother incubated his interest in the natural world by sharing her extensive knowledge of wildflowers. Self-taught, she knew all the scientific names of almost all the plants in the mountains. McMillan studied biology at the University of North Carolina in Chapel Hill and then earned a PhD in biological sciences at Clemson University. His specialty is botany, but his knowledge of the natural world extends far beyond plants. He studies the complex web of life and how one missing strand can make the whole weaker. Blond and boyish, McMillan has an engaging manner that makes his listener want to hear what he has to say, and he uses his magnetism to educate people about the importance of biodiversity. He advances his message with speaking engagements and seminars, as well as for Educational Television's *Expeditions with Patrick McMillan*, which he hosts, co-created and helps write. He also teaches at Clemson University, where he directs operations at the Campbell Museum of Natural History.

He recalls the first time he laid eyes on the Chattooga River, a view from Bull Pen Road, when he was about twelve years old: "Incredible. I was struck, walking through the forest with old-man's beard lichen hanging from huge trees, with the feeling that everything was…" he pauses, searching for the precise word, "saturated." He was on a quest for the filmy fern, which eluded him. Many years later, he finally found his quarry during another visit to the river, near the Highway 28 Bridge. The filmy fern is so called because it is only one cell-layer thick, its leaves almost transparent. This fragile plant underlines the importance of the Blue Ridge Escarpment, shaped by the Chattooga River. First of all, this fern is an entirely tropical family, yet four species of it have made their way out of the tropics and into the escarpment. They live in what McMillan describes as an eighty-five-mile swath, or eco-region, the only place in North America you can find all four species of this fern. Two are found only in the escarpment.

This amazing translocation is possible because the gorges are sheltered, McMillan continues. The air is always cooler in these nooks in the summer and warmer in the winter, for several reasons: the wind can't penetrate these sheltered coves, the sun can't shine directly into them and water acts as an insulator of sorts. You might wonder how the filmy ferns found their way to these coves in the first place all the way from the tropics. The answer is that their spores are light enough to be borne along on upper wind currents, transporting them to the mountains, where they drifted down into the little pockets of microclimate, safe from the extremes of temperature. The fact that the fern is so fragile yet managed to survive ice ages in the area further illustrates the importance of these coves; likewise, the fact that the fern now is disappearing is cause for alarm. McMillan estimates that 90 percent of them have died in the last decade because of the "pervasive and dramatic drought, the like of which we've never seen in recorded history. Something happened in just the past decade that has to do with weather." While the drought has eased, for now, its occurrence underscores the unpredictability of the climate and how change may threaten some unique and fragile habitats and their inhabitants.

The Chattooga drains the escarpment, enabling it to offer a highway, in addition to sheltering coves. "Plant and animal distribution tends to follow watersheds, and some follow the corridor all the way down to the fall line," says McMillan. In past ages, when the climate got colder, species would move gradually down the mountain; as it warmed, they would move back to higher elevations. These events happened slowly so that most species, including plants (excepting trilliums), were able to escape in the right direction, and those that couldn't move were protected in their pockets of microclimate. Currently, however, the climate is becoming warmer and drier, an occurrence that has not happened often, so plants with limited distribution and dispersal are in danger of becoming imperiled. The trillium, the filmy fern and the Oconee bell may have nowhere to go, even if they can, unless their ecosystems remain intact and connected as in the past. Plants are not the only organisms at risk if the climate warms. The wood frog, which is found as far north as the Arctic, is at its southernmost range in the watershed and could be pushed out if the average temperature becomes too warm to support it.

In short, the Chattooga River corridor "may be the most important piece of land in eastern North America, the most important piece of landscape for preserving life" through the changes to come, says McMillan. "We sit on the precipice of change, so where better to have something protected that can provide us with a future?" The problem is that "we're heading into uncharted territory. My hope is that the Southern Blue Ridge Escarpment and the Chattooga River will function as in the past," providing both an escape and a refuge for the environs and dwellers within.

Dangerous Invaders

The Chattooga River watershed is incredibly diverse, home to many species of plants, including, of course, trees. "It's a typical Appalachian forest, but it's almost archetypal, an example of the best, maybe on the planet," says naturalist Patrick McMillan. You can find "more species of trees in one cove than you can in some European countries." However, danger lurks in the forest. Not panthers, as some people have, erroneously, reported seeing; these big cats haven't existed there for years. This danger has many emissaries that can stealthily enter a forest and wreak havoc. They sometimes kill outright, as the blight did the American chestnut; sometimes they out-compete native species, as does the fire ant. They are other invasive species, often simply referred to as "invasives."

Currently, the most notorious invasive is the wooly adelgid, which is decimating the eastern hemlock throughout the Appalachian forests. The quiet coves of the Chattooga watershed have become graveyards, filled with the skeletal remains of these evergreens. The culprit was introduced into the United States through Japan by way of the New York Botanical Gardens, which had imported Japanese hemlock for its collection. The foreign version was resistant to the wooly adelgid, a small sap-sucking insect related to the aphid, because host and parasite co-evolved; as tree developed resistance to parasite, parasite developed a way to extract sap without killing tree. The eastern hemlock has no defense against the adelgid. A bug that resembles a tiny speck of dryer lint, and looks as insignificant, is destroying an entire species of tree. "Another chapter in the globalization and loss of species

Left: Healthy hemlock trees. *Photo by Dr. Ed Pivorun.*

Right: Hemlock trees killed by the wooly adelgid. *Photo by Dr. Ed Pivorun.*

and the homogenization of the world," McMillan laments, speaking to the law of unintended consequences when humans introduce exotic species into places they don't belong.

In a study conducted in 2009, researchers "predict a complete loss of the hemlock forest type within 20 years of adelgid establishment," resulting in "denser deciduous forests with thinner canopies and multiple gaps, and significant alterations to terrestrial and aquatic wildlife habitat." Heather L. Spaulding and Lynne K. Rieske explain, in an article for the journal *Biological Invasions*, that the hemlock plays a crucial role in creating and maintaining "unique microclimate conditions by regulating air and stream temperatures," as well as soil chemistry. Disturbance of these conditions has an impact on wildlife, such as white-tailed deer, which browse on hemlock sprouts. According to a University of Rhode Island fact sheet, the wooly adelgid kills the hemlock by sucking its sap and "probably also by injecting a toxic saliva while feeding," causing the needles and buds to dry up and fall off. After being defoliated, the trees are rendered sterile. The mortality rate is 95 percent or greater, report Spaulding and Rieske.

The adelgid, first documented in 1951, began a very rapid and aggressive expansion in the mid-1980s, spreading through the air and via nursery stock. So far, no defenses are available, but efforts to find some are underway. While several options have been studied, they yield mixed results because their application is not viable for densely forested areas. These include the application of horticultural oils or pesticides, as well as a combination of insects that prey on the adelgid. The Forest Service states, "It will likely take a complex of natural enemies to maintain hemlock wooly adelgid populations below damaging levels."

Another imminent threat to trees, including those in the Chattooga watershed, is the emerald ash borer, also from Asia. "If you know where to find an ash tree, go look at it, because in five years it'll be gone," advises McMillan. This insect lives up to its name, adorned with brilliant, metallic-green wings, a pinkish abdomen and a penchant for drilling holes into the wood of ash trees. About half an inch long, this beetle is a small, beautiful killer. So why not just douse affected trees with insecticide? Because then the beneficials—insects that facilitate pollination and seed dispersal—become casualties also.

The list of invasives continues: ambrosia beetles kill trees in the laurel family; sudden-oak death takes out these venerable old hardwoods; and the herald of spring, the dogwood, has been knocked out of most of the Appalachians by a fungal pest. All these changes are driven by humans. "You wonder what's going to be left," says McMillan. Efforts are underway to address the problem through the creation of a website called "Don't Move Firewood." The campaign was designed to raise public awareness and disseminate information about the spread of invasive forest pests, which include dozens of insects and pathogens. The website, owned by the Nature Conservancy, was developed based on dialogues among a group of organizations and people determined to take action "to abate the threat to North American forests from non-native insects and diseases." The idea is simple: to prevent the spread of pests, don't move firewood.

Invasives are a problem not just in the Chattooga River watershed but also all over the country. The python was introduced to the swamps of Florida, where the snake thrives, by irresponsible pet owners who release them when they get bored caring for them. The grass carp escaped from ornamental ponds and found their way into the Mississippi River, where they move inexorably toward the Great Lakes. The zebra mussel already resides in these great bodies of water, dropped off the hulls of incoming ships and now out-competing the native mussels, disrupting the food chain and clogging water intakes and boat motors. Another invasive, which was spread by humans but now is extinct in the wild, decimated the Native American population when introduced by white settlers: smallpox.

A forest without any trees is a horrible thought—in fact, it would not even be a forest—before considering one of the most-hated invasives: fire ants. So called for good reason, they secretly mass upon their victim, hold themselves in position with their mandibles and begin to sting painfully and repeatedly after giving a chemical communication start signal to the others. You don't know you're covered with fire ants until all ten, or one thousand or ten thousand, start biting and stinging. They are extremely aggressive, at the least disturbance exploding like living lava from their volcano-shaped mounds. Their venom causes the eruption of pustules that burn and itch for days, even weeks. They can cause allergic reaction, and even death, to humans, wild animals and livestock. They routinely kill helpless creatures they encounter, such as baby quails or turtles, as well as anything else that can't run away. In an apocryphal story, a deer hunter fell out of a stand, was knocked unconscious and had the bad luck to land on a fire ant mound. He died from the effects of tens of thousands of stings.

Fire ants, an exotic invasive species, swarm from their nest at the slightest provocation. *Photo by Dr. Ed Pivorun.*

A Natural and Cultural History

The fire ant invasion started between 1918 and 1930, hitting the Southeast around the 1980s. Accidentally introduced from South America, they are found in Louisiana, Florida and South Carolina and parts of Texas, Oklahoma, Arkansas, Mississippi, Alabama, Georgia and North Carolina, according to "Fire Ant History." They aren't found in high numbers in the mountains because they like sunny, open spaces as opposed to trees and shade. "If you need a reason to keep an area roadless, that's it, because roads provide a highway for fire ants," cautions McMillan. Fire ants are a bane for native ants, out-competing and displacing them. They then take over trillium seeds, with a sinister twist: instead of eating the part of the seed that acts as a sort of ant bait and then dropping the seed to germinate, the fire ants take the seed back to their nests. There, they either eat the entire seed, leaving nothing to germinate, or leave it to languish in the nest—in the sunny areas fire ants require but where trillium cannot grow. McMillan warns, "Fire ants could stop the dispersion of native spring wildflowers."

Insects are not the only invasives to worry about. Nonnative invasive plants also can move in and displace the natives. "Everyone worries about kudzu, which is not invasive; it only grows on edges," says McMillan. Instead, we should focus on such threats as Chinese privet, Japanese honeysuckle and English ivy; none is a problem yet, but they all could become so. In addition, invasive animals, including feral hogs, can be found in the watershed. Recently, McMillan saw an armadillo trundling along the side of a mountain road.

Invasive species drive out natives, reducing diversity and upsetting a delicate balance that has taken eons to develop. In come fire ants, out go wildflowers; in come wooly adelgids, out go hemlocks. Everything is connected, and every action has a consequence. McMillan's advice seems simple: "Minimize the amount of human-driven disturbance." Don't introduce any nonnative species, of any kind, where they don't belong. They may bring wholesale destruction with them, as they have in the not-so-long-ago.

A Fungus Among Us

In 1904, a killer came to this country from Asia, disembarking in New York City and traveling down the East Coast. Slaughtering billions, this stealthy mass murderer did not stop until it had destroyed an entire race. The perpetrator? A fungus. Its victim? The American chestnut. By 1950, the tree was virtually extinct in the wild after being ravaged by the chestnut blight (*Cryphonectria parasitica*), which was brought into the United States by accident from Asia. An estimated four billion American chestnuts, representing one-quarter of the standing trees in the Appalachian forest, were wiped out. The good news is that modern science is being employed to fight the blight and restore the American chestnut. The bad news is that the blight is not the only threat to the tree.

The range of the American chestnut stretched from Maine to the Deep South and across the Carolina Piedmont to the Ohio Valley. A full-grown American chestnut tree was an impressive sight, possessing a tall, straight trunk reaching up to one hundred feet and five to twelve feet in diameter. Its slender, tapering leaves were edged with what look like breaking waves. In the spring, the tree sported flowering tassels of cream, called catkins, that produced a bur, a small hand of spines that fisted around the nuts and protected them from marauding squirrels. Most burs opened while still on the tree, raining down the tiny brown shells. Concealing sweet meat, the pinball-sized chestnuts were prized by wildlife and humans. In the fall, they carpeted the ground, providing mast for deer, turkeys, squirrels, raccoons and other wildlife. Native Americans depended on them, using the leaves for

The American chestnut tree, now virtually extinct, once was the dominant species in the Appalachians. *Photo courtesy of The American Chestnut Foundation.*

medical remedies and the nuts for eating and for grinding into flour. When white settlers discovered the trees' bounty, farmers learned to release their livestock into the woods to forage, saving them the expense of feed (and possibly supporting a population of invasive feral hogs). They also collected bushels of the nuts to eat (think "chestnuts roasting on an open fire") and to trade for store-bought goods.

A fast grower, the American chestnut was the dominant hardwood in its range. Heavily logged, its straightness made for easy splitting by hand, and its wood was extremely resistant to decay. It was used to build houses, fences and furniture, as well as utility poles, railroad ties and mine support shafts; the tannins produced by the wood were used for tanning leather. White settlers also came to depend on it heavily for all the benefits it offered.

The tree's popularity was demonstrated, among other ways, by the high incidence of place names containing "chestnut": streets, roads, towns, churches, geographical locations and cemeteries. Like the passenger pigeon, the tree was so plentiful its demise was unimaginable. So when the chestnut trees started to die, and the horrific thought dawned that the tree might disappear, forces of science and government mustered in an attempt to save it. However, the tree's fate had been sealed the day a foreign chestnut tree, bearing an invisible pathogen, was imported. It spread through water, by riding air currents and by hitching a ride on a bird, squirrel or pant leg. Big orange cankers, the sign of blight, erupted on tree after tree like grotesque blossoms as the disease spread inexorably south.

If anyone needs a cautionary tale about the dangers of introducing invasive species into a new environment, they need look no further than the American chestnut. In less than fifty years, billions of trees blanketing millions of acres were gone because a chestnut from Asia was brought into the United States. The Asian trees, having coevolved over millions of years with this fungus, had developed resistance; after all, if a pathogen destroys its host, it cannot survive. The American chestnut, however, had no resistance because it never had encountered this disease, and the chestnut blight swept through the Southeast, killing every tree it infected.

Perhaps feeling a collective guilt over the death of the American chestnut, a few determined individuals refused to accept that it was gone forever. Efforts to restore the American chestnut are underway and have been, intermittently, for decades. In the 1930s and 1940s, several large-scale attempts were made to breed a blight-resistant tree, but they were unsuccessful and were abandoned by the 1960s. However, in 1983, scientists began using a method that had been successful in battling diseases in wheat and corn, using the pollen and seeds from earlier efforts. In addition, they collected from wild trees; although the blight decimated all the centuries-old, massive trees that dominated the forest, American chestnuts do still grow in the wild. The tree is able to coppice—in other words, regenerate itself from its roots—if the main trunk is killed by blight (or chopped down). These sprouts usually die from the blight before they are able to reproduce; however, on occasion they manage to grow old enough to reach sexual maturity. At this point, they can produce seeds and pollen before dying of the fungus.

The first serious modern attempt to breed blight-resistant American chestnut trees began in the 1980s, at Meadowview Research Farms in Virginia, and continues today. The orchard is owned by The American Chestnut Foundation (TACF), whose mission is to restore the tree to its former range and viability. TACF scientists use backcrossing, a technique that allows scientists to breed resistance forward while gradually diluting unwanted characteristics. The purpose is to breed a chestnut that is as American as possible while retaining the blight resistance of the Chinese tree. First, American chestnuts are crossed with their Chinese cousins and then assessed for resistance. Those that show the most promise are backcrossed with other American chestnuts until they are 94 percent American, which takes three generations. Since the goal is to produce a tree that retains the Chinese gene for blight resistance, at this point scientists infect them with blight to determine which ones have done so.

Selecting for blight resistance is only one front in the battle to restore the American chestnut, however. Joe James is more worried about slime mold than blight. *Phytophthora cinnamomi* is its scientific designation, and James contends that it poses as much danger to the restored American chestnut as does the blight, at least in the southern end of the chestnut's range. His task has become to try to breed American chestnut trees that are resistant to *Phytophthora* as well as to the blight. A retired orthopedist, James lives in the countryside of Seneca, South Carolina, in a large white Victorian-style home with green shutters. An expansive front porch overlooks a field of winter wheat, green and full of the promise of spring. The Blue Ridge Escarpment, once dominated by the American chestnut, rises in the distance. In James's backyard is a fenced area containing rows of plastic, livestock-watering troughs, in which he plants chestnut seeds. In another row are three-gallon buckets with chestnut saplings about eighteen inches high, awaiting their turn to be planted in the field. He calls his place "Chestnut Return."

James has a wonderful bedside manner. He is focused, attentive, detail oriented, knowledgeable, indefatigable and determined to save his patient, the American chestnut. He uses artificial selection, and, as in natural selection, the weak must die—a necessary sacrifice. James is condensing the evolutionary process by breeding trees, infecting them with *Phytophthora* and planting the survivors in buckets and then, when they are three years old, in a field on his property. He loses about 95 percent but is certain that one day he will breed a *Phytophthora*-resistant tree. During a conversation about his work, James relaxes in a wicker rocking chair on his porch and puffs a cigar. He got interested in the American chestnut in the late 1980s and read as much as he could about the tree. He kept thinking it was such a shame it had been wiped out, albeit unintentionally, by humans. He wanted to do something.

James once found one of those rare surviving trees that somehow had avoided the blight and grown to sexual maturity. "It was exhilarating," he recalls. He alerted Meadowview, and scientists came to collect seeds and pollen from the tree to add to their stock of breeding material, enlarging the gene pool and ensuring genetic variability. "Trees must have significant genetic diversity to survive in the wild, so our scientists are always adding new material to the breeding program," explains Paul Franklin, former director of communications for TACF. New gene combinations allow individuals to adapt to new circumstances; without genetic diversity, populations cannot evolve.

Meanwhile, James had begun raising American chestnuts, which were dying, but not from blight. The killer, *Phytophthora*, was another invasive species, brought over in the mid- to late 1700s, when Charleston planters were attempting to grow exotic plant species such as olives and avocados. *Phytophthora* is nondiscriminatory, attacking more than one thousand trees of all species, and is spread by water, in pots or on the soles of shoes. It gradually made its way up from the coast into the Upstate but cannot survive where ground freezes solid and therefore cannot establish a roothold in the mountains. James speculates that the American chestnut had an even larger range than is believed but was wiped out in lower latitudes by *Phytophthora* before the tree's historic range was mapped.

In the field where he plants his trees, James pulls up an ailing sapling, shakes the dirt off and whittles a bit of bark away to decipher the message written by *Phytophthora*, known also as ink disease: black streaks staining the inner layers of tissue from the root up. In another row, a couple of saplings have grown up to about seven feet. One looks healthy, with glowing brownish-red bark; the other has a gray cast, and James predicts that it is dying. Once *Phytophthora* finds a host, it "grows like crazy," attacking the roots of the tree, blocking the absorption of water. The tree dies, horribly, of thirst. James began trying to convince other scientists that *Phytophthora* was a serious threat to restoration efforts but was not taken seriously at first. After all, he was a medical doctor, not a plant pathologist. However, through his efforts, James gradually won over his doubters and recently was vindicated; in 2007, he was presented the Man of the Year Award by TACF. James uses the same backcrossing technique as TACF in his battle against *Phytophthora*. His objectives are to find an American chestnut that can fight off both *Phytophthora* and the blight and become a "nut-producing seed orchard."

In 2005, TACF scientists announced that they had harvested the first potentially blight-resistant chestnut seeds, and currently, the American chestnut is being reintroduced to the Appalachian Mountains. The Forest Service has planted about five thousand saplings in various "undisclosed locations" above the current range of *Phytophthora*. Paul Franklin says he's hesitant to say it's blight resistant, but James is more optimistic, asserting, "If humans left the planet tomorrow, the trees would repopulate." In any event, TACF soon will begin large-scale planting of what it hopes will be blight-resistant trees in the wild. "The effort to restore the American chestnut is almost entirely driven by its membership and volunteers," says Franklin, adding that TACF welcomes new members who would enjoy helping bring back this species from the brink of extinction.

Although at first James used his own money to fund his efforts, he now receives support in the form of grants from TACF. Still, his desire to restore the American chestnut is so intense that he probably would continue his work even if he had to pay for it himself. "They're like children in a way," he says of the trees in his charge. With luck and continued hard work, James will send the nuts produced by his "tree children" out into the world to sprout a brave new world of American chestnuts. He won't live long enough to see them reach adulthood, but maybe his human grandchildren will. One day they may sit, backs against the trunk of an American chestnut tree, enjoying the shade and the sweet meat of a chestnut. And who knows? Maybe that American chestnut will be one of the ones born and raised on their grandfather's farm.

Attack of the White-Nose Syndrome

The much-maligned bat actually is harmless—unless you're an insect. In fact, bats are very beneficial. A colony of these flying mammals can consume tens of thousands of mosquitoes a night. Bats also eat other pestiferous insects, such as those that attack crops and ravage fruit trees, and they act as pollinators and seed dispersers. Perhaps their nefarious reputation arose because they are creatures of the night, the consorts of vampires, lurking in dark, dank caves. Actually, only three species of bats drink blood, and they live in the tropics of Central and South America, not Romania. Furthermore, according to Bat Conservation International (BCI), vampire bats more closely resemble kittens drinking milk than raving sanguisuges. They also have medical uses: the anti-clotting enzyme in their saliva is used as a treatment in stroke.

More than 1,200 species of bats compose about one-fifth of all mammals. They range from the size of a bumblebee to that of a fox with a six-foot wingspan and inhabit all but the hottest desert and coldest pole. They feed primarily on insects but also on fruit and seeds. Some bats eat frogs, fish, mice and other small animals, hunting at night, using sonar to locate their prey. Appearances vary wildly and reflect eating habits. The lesser long-nosed bat looks like the devil's minion, with hornlike ears and a pointy nose; however, it sups innocently on cactus nectar, made easier by its tapered proboscis. The spotted bat has translucent Dumbo ears that enable it to hear and capture its favored food: moths. Chapin's free-tailed bat has a mohawk, and the white fruit bat looks like a cotton ball with wings. The Gambian epauletted fruit bat has an endearing expression, with large liquid eyes and small, pointed ears giving it the placating attitude of a friendly dog. Once you look at their photos, it's hard to bear them ill will.

Bats flit through the Chattooga River corridor, scooping up moths and other insects by night, sleeping in trees or caves by day. Mary Bunch, a mammologist for SC DNR, is worried about them. She's afraid they will fall victim to white-nose syndrome, which is spreading through bat populations in the southeastern United States and parts of the Midwest and has killed an estimated 5.7 million bats—about as many people as live in Atlanta. So far, the *Geomyces destructans* fungus has been found in the tri-colored bat and the small-footed bat in Pickens County, which is adjacent to Oconee County in South Carolina. First noted in 2006 in a recreational cave in New York State, white-nose syndrome is thought to be European, transported to this country on caving equipment. The species was new to science by the time it was named in 2009, two years after it began to kill bats. Bunch explains, "The way it has rapidly spread and decimated bats is a pretty good indicator that our bats are naïve," meaning that the bats have no immunity to this exotic invasive species.

Like another exotic invasive, the hemlock wooly adelgid, white-nose syndrome looks innocuous, like a bit of white fluff stuck on the bat's nose. However, also like the adelgid, white-nose is insidious and ultimately fatal to its host. It grows on the bat's skin, causing the wing membrane to break down. "A bat's wing is of critical importance for thermal regulation and elasticity for flight," says Bunch in a telephone interview. The syndrome affects only the colonial hibernating bat species, although not all the bats in this category. The unfortunates are bats that induce torpor in cold months, which is more effective for them than staying active in order to hunt. However, because their immune system is not as active in this state, they are vulnerable to white-nose syndrome. "They shut down the blood supply to the peripheral areas, and the fungus takes advantage of that," says Bunch. If they are exposed for a long time, she says, they end up starving to death because by the time they come out of hibernation, they can't fly; or the fungus causes them to come out of hibernation too soon and they starve or freeze to death. "It's sad to see these poor animals flopping around on the ground," dehydrated and starving, she says. Unfortunately, the fungus is spreading rapidly, and no cure is known. "The disease is moving faster than the science," Bunch says. "Extirpation of some species is being predicted."

Of the nine species of bats in the Chattooga River watershed, the five that might be affected by white-nose syndrome include the little brown bat, the northern long-eared bat, the small-footed bat, the big brown bat and the tri-colored bat, which Bunch describes as "real cute, nifty little bats." They are the first to enter hibernation and the last to leave, which means they are exposed for a long time, making them very vulnerable to the syndrome. It's hard to check them for fungus, she says, because as they roost they become covered with condensation. The frosting of water droplets mimics the fungus and makes it hard to see. Another complicating factor is that, being small and able to fly, bats are hard to find. "We don't always know where they are," she says, which can make it hard to determine if they have the fungus. A colony lives at the Walhalla Fish Hatchery, and Bunch has attached transmitters to some individuals. She says she hasn't seen any sign of fungus there but is afraid that, in time, she will. The fungus spreads bat to bat, as well as on caving equipment and on the wind. The good news is that "we won't lose all our bats to it." The syndrome is not known in tree bats or in non-hibernating bats, because these bats are more active, meaning their immune systems are more robust. "If the bat is awake, it's fighting the fungus," Bunch explains. In addition, some southeastern hibernating bats may be safe because they over-winter in buildings, where the temperature is too warm for the fungus, which thrives in cool, damp environments.

Bats sometimes are disproportionately associated with rabies, a virus that is 100 percent fatal if untreated. However, according to the Centers for Disease Control, most of the cases of wildlife rabies are found in raccoons, followed by skunks. To avoid exposure, never approach a wild animal, especially one that seems sick or aggressive. Wild animals that show no fear of humans may be sick and should be reported to the state DNR or an animal control entity. Pets should be vaccinated annually, since most human exposure comes from dogs and cats. Outdoor cats are especially vulnerable, as they have more contact with potential carriers. Bats sometimes roost in buildings and occasionally will accidentally end up in a house. These are not necessarily rabid, however; bats will not attack and in fact are quite shy. They definitely won't fly into your hair, at least not deliberately. If you decide to remove the bat yourself, leave a window open and interior doors shut; the bat most likely will fly out on its own. If that doesn't work, put a box over the bat and then slip a piece of cardboard underneath so that the bat is trapped. Wait until dark and then take the bat outside and release it. If it doesn't fly away, it may be sick or injured; call DNR or animal control.

In short, these winged kittens won't drink your blood but can stop other entities from doing so. So don't be afraid to sit outside at dusk and look for little silhouettes fluttering about. Watch in wonder as these voracious little creatures swoop and dive, devouring the real bloodsuckers.

Hog Versus Coyote

Despite what some people think, the feral hog is a nuisance and the coyote is not. These people, who most likely are hunters, are wrong. They simply aren't in possession of the facts. Fact: the feral hog is an exotic (as in not native to this country) invasive species that degrades habitat, competes with other wildlife and spreads disease. Fact: the coyote does none of these things. Both animals take an occasional white-tailed deer fawn, but for some reason only the coyote is demonized for it while the hog is not. But if a hunter fails to bag a deer, does he blame his own lack of marksmanship? More than likely, not; instead, he vilifies the coyote. However, peruse the Wild Hog Task Force website for a photograph of a giant hog ravaging the mutilated carcass of a fawn.

However, convincing the detractors that coyotes aren't rampaging through the forest, slaughtering deer, is difficult. A certain type of person refuses to accept a conclusion he—and this person usually is a he—disagrees with, no matter how much evidence supports it. This type is likely to dismiss the findings of experts, for instance wildlife biologists, who have studied the complex interactions of wildlife and the environment. Because he's a hunter, this type believes he knows more about the woods than "them educated types." He tends not to look at the whole, as opposed to just the part that affects him or that he perceives affects him. He likes to hunt hogs; therefore, hogs are good. Just ignore the fact that they sometimes kill white-tailed fawns. On the other hand, says Greg Yarrow, "If one coyote kills and eats a white-tailed deer that a hunter *could have gotten* [his emphasis], that's one coyote too many."

While not native to the South, the coyote has slipped into a niche formerly occupied by native predators, the wolf and the cougar, which were extirpated by man. "They fit the classic definition of an opportunistic omnivore," says Yarrow, a wildlife biologist and the chair of the Natural Resources Division at Clemson University. However, "they're going to expend the least amount of energy for the most gain," which means easiest prey, which deer are not. Furthermore, coyotes don't hunt in packs, so it simply doesn't make sense for them to waste energy hunting big prey and risk being injured in the process. Yarrow, who has been with Clemson for twenty-five years but somehow looks only forty, specializes in human-wildlife conflicts. He points out that, while coyotes are found statewide and do contribute to fawn mortality in South Carolina, the deer population is capable of absorbing it: 750,000, according to a 2012 report by the SC DNR. So if a hunter can't bag one deer out of all the hundreds of thousands galloping around the state, it's probably not because coyotes are the better hunters. If deer numbers do fall and, as a result, deer become more difficult to kill, coyotes switch to smaller food items: grasshoppers, blackberries and even feral piglets (one hopes). In short, Yarrow doesn't see coyotes having much of an impact on deer numbers, pointing out that some states (Texas, for example) that have had coyotes for years "still have too many deer." Recently, he was startled to discover that SC DNR is running a campaign, "Hunters: Help Control Coyotes, Save Our Deer," which encourages them to shoot the canines on sight. When he asked someone at the agency why the campaign was initiated, he was told it was a political decision, illustrating that elected officials often make policy on matters in which they are not expert.

Meanwhile, consider the feral hog, which Yarrow calls "the biggest conservation challenge in terms of a problem species." The feral hog was introduced by explorers and white settlers during the colonization of America and easily established a hoof-hold in this land of plenty. Not only are they ubiquitous to the South, they are prolific. The females can start breeding at six months and have two to three litters of seven to twelve piglets each year. "They traditionally stay around watersheds, like the Chattooga River," he adds, where they can cause significant habitat destruction through rooting. Hogs destroy sensitive plant communities, as well as isolated wetlands that support rare amphibians, which they eat. In addition, hogs can cause siltation in streambeds, which raises the water temperature and can result in trout mortality. They also present a danger to domestic animals through the potential spread of brucellosis and foot-and-mouth disease, says Yarrow. Like the coyote, they are opportunistic

Feral hogs are an exotic invasive species that destroy habitat and kill native species like white-tailed deer and endangered salamanders. *Photo courtesy of John Kilgo, United States Forest Service.*

omnivores, only destructive. They can grow to four-hundred-plus pounds—a lot of hog doing a lot of damage.

One of the reasons the feral hog challenge is so great is that people like to hunt them, so they overlook, or choose to ignore, the pernicious impact of the animal. Hog hunting is legal all year round, day or night. Moving hogs around the state, or over state lines, is illegal, although people regularly engage in this activity. The Wild Hog Task Force, a coalition of state and federal agencies, non-government and conservation groups, is an effort by Clemson University to manage the problem. The objectives of the task force are to develop, issue and publish guidelines; assess and monitor wild hog population; conduct a risk assessment regarding potential spread of wild hog populations; support legislation addressing wild hog management; and develop a statewide management plan. The website for the task force features

Coyotes do not hunt in packs and therefore are not able to have a significant impact on white-tailed deer populations. *Photo courtesy of John Kilgo, United States Forest Service.*

an electronic form for reporting sightings of wild hogs, as well as photos of the animal at work. One shows a gigantic, hairy, black monster of a hog standing with one foot on a dead lamb, slurping blood and entrails. Another shows the impact of a wild hog or hogs on an agricultural site: the ground, and the corn growing on it, has been churned into soup. A close-up of a hog's face illustrates how it can wreak such incredible damage, with a long, thick snout framed by sharp, hooked tusks. Tiny eyes gleam intelligently out of coarse brown fur.

The wild hog contributes nothing to the environment, from the standpoint of a biologist, but does cause a lot of damage. The only thing in the wild hog's favor is that some people like to hunt it. "On balance, not a good reason to keep them around," concludes Yarrow, who adds that they may prove hard to eradicate because they breed so promiscuously and are a popular game species. He can only hope that the task force can help raise awareness and educate people about the damage this species, which doesn't belong here, is doing to the environment. Maybe one day, people who like to hunt wild hogs will realize that the environment as a whole is worth more than the short-lived thrill of bagging one of these animals. And maybe they'll stop blaming the coyote for their own lack of hunting skill.

The Chattooga River provides a natural highway for birds. *Photo by Peter McIntosh.*

A black-and-white warbler trills from a tree branch. *Photo by Dr. Ed Pivorun.*

Left: The actor Ronny Cox, also a musician/songwriter, played the doomed Drew in the movie *Deliverance*. *Photo by Laura A. Garren.*

Below: Rafters disappear under a spume of white water. *Photo by Ethan Monk of Southeastern Expeditions.*

Opposite, top: Rafters enjoy the excitement of running rapids on a Wild and Scenic River. *Photo by Ethan Monk of Southeastern Expeditions.*

Opposite, bottom: A white-water fishing spider poses on a rock. *Photo by L.L. Gaddy.*

A large rainbow trout caught in the Chattooga River above Licklog Creek. *Photo by Laura A. Garren.*

The beautiful brook trout has been restored to several tributaries of the Chattooga. *Photo by Karen Breedlove Chastain.*

An angler tries his luck at Three Forks. *Photo by Reis Birdwhistell.*

The mitten crawfish is so named because of its fuzzy, oversized claws. *Photo by Chris Lukhaup.*

A hiking trail carpeted with rhododendron petals. *Photo by Peter McIntosh.*

King Creek Falls is one of many cascades in the Chattooga River watershed. *Photo by Peter McIntosh.*

Fall colors enliven the river. *Photo by Peter McIntosh.*

Trilliums thrive in the Chattooga River watershed and surrounding environs. *Photo by Reis Birdwhistell.*

The spotted salamander is the South Carolina State Amphibian. *Photo by Dr. Ed Pivorun.*

The Oconee bell is native to the gorges of the Blue Ridge Escarpment but has been transplanted to the Chattooga River watershed. *Photo by Dr. Ed Pivorun.*

The wood frog is found in the Chattooga River watershed and as far north as the Arctic. *Photo by Dr. Ed Pivorun.*

The wooly adelgid is decimating eastern hemlocks and is expected to wipe them out completely within twenty years. *Photo by Dr. Ed Pivorun.*

The leaves of the American chestnut tree curl along their edges. *Photo courtesy of The American Chestnut Foundation.*

The catkin, or pollen tassel, of an American chestnut tree. *Photo courtesy of The American Chestnut Foundation.*

The burr of the American chestnut tree is protected by a casing of spines. *Photo courtesy of The American Chestnut Foundation.*

Bats feed voraciously on mosquitoes; a single colony can consume thousands during a single feeding. *Photo by Dr. Ed Pivorun.*

Opposite, top: A black bear, woozy after sedation, peeks through the brush. *Photo by Skip Still.*

Opposite, bottom: Peter Peteet (right) and Buzz Williams discuss the removal of a 250-year-old canoe that Peteet found in the Chattooga River. On the left is Dr. Chris Amer, an underwater anthropologist with the South Carolina Institute of Archeology and Anthropology, who advised Williams and other Chattooga Conservancy volunteers in the removal of the canoe. *Photo courtesy of the Chattooga Conservancy.*

Above: An aerial view of the site of Chattooga Town, an old Cherokee village. *Photo by Gerald Schroedl.*

Right: Kayakers paddle below Singley Falls against a palette of fall colors. *Photo by Reis Birdwhistell.*

Barriers erected across part of the upper Chattooga River that runs through private property. *Photo by Kevin Colburn.*

Meanwhile, the river runs. *Photo by Peter McIntosh.*

The Right to Arm Bears

D eer kill more people than bears do, according to Skip Still. He ought to know, having been a bear biologist for SC DNR for thirty years. Of course, these deer-related deaths are caused by collisions with automobiles. The point is that black bears generally are of no danger to humans. However, they are opportunistic omnivores, which means they'll eat almost anything: garbage, dog food, birdseed and myriad irresistible treats associated with human habitation. Their pillaging can irritate some people, who want to live in nature's backyard but don't want nature *in* their backyards.

The Chattooga River watershed is home to a growing, healthy population of black bears. Still, who retired in 2009, estimates one per square mile. Furthermore, the biggest bears come out of Oconee County, he says; the biggest bear in state record, weighing 594 pounds, was killed there. But how do you figure out how many bears are in the woods? Send out census surveys? Still, his eyes twinkling over a mischievous grin and a robust mustache, explains. He and fellow biologists string barbed wire (pronounced by him as "bob wire") to trees, forming a square; in the middle, they hang lures (feminine sanitary napkins, of all things) soaked in raspberry extract. As a reward, they also leave a bag of donuts. When a bear walks under the wire, bits of fur are snagged by the barbs. The collected fur is then used to extract genetic information about the bears, such as how many actually passed through the square, as well as the gender and the relationships amongst them. Once the biologists had access to this DNA technology, they found out that they had grossly underestimated the numbers. Before, Still says, they estimated that about fifty bears lived in the watershed; after, they found out the population was closer to one thousand. "We were way off," he understates. In the past, bears were tranquilized before being assessed, a stressful experience for the animal; the fur-capture method obviates the need for trapping. "Unfortunately, we can't tell the health of the bear" using the DNA study, Still rues. While he talks, he clicks on photographs on his computer: bears. With no scale for contrast, how big is this bear or that one? Look at the ears, Still explains: if they're small and tucked, the bear is a big adult; large and pointy, the bear is small and probably a youngster. He illustrates with a photo of what looks like a massive bear coming out of a tranquilizer-induced stupor. Tiny ears? Yes. Big bear. "This one would probably go 400, 450 pounds," says Still. Another, looking dazedly at the camera, has large, cartoonish ears. He's much smaller and has what looks like a sweet, if clueless, expression on his face.

So, lots of bears live in the woods surrounding the Chattooga, doing what they do, which is mostly foraging. Most of their diet consists of berries and fruit, including oak mast, supplemented with meat in the form of yellow jackets and an occasional fawn or hog. (If you have visions of a bear scooping trout out of the river, you're imagining Alaska, salmon and grizzlies.) When they're about three years old, females breed in the spring, and six months later they give birth. Unlike bears that live in colder climes, black bears don't go into full hibernation mode; instead, says Still, they enter a torpid state. During this semi-hibernation, they give birth to two to four tiny cubs. When the family emerges in early spring, the mother teaches her offspring everything she knows and starts encouraging independence after about a year.

Bears are generally shy and afraid of humans—also dogs. In fact, Still knows of an incident in which a Chihuahua treed a bear. Unfortunately, he did not get a picture. However, bears can become acclimated to humans, especially when food is involved. The best meal is the easiest, to a bear, so they will take advantage of garbage and other human comestibles. In one complaint, a bear "picked up a fifty-pound bag of dog food and just walked off," Still recalls. As a state bear biologist, he routinely dealt with people who had loose garbage or an unfenced garden or beehive and wondered why a bear treated it as an all-you-can-eat buffet. Often, people would expect him to remove the bear, but he got "good at saying, 'No.'" Solutions are simple: put a bungee cord across the lid of the garbage bin, store dog food securely, "Don't leave a freezer out on the porch." (Duh!) Once they understand, many people cooperate, but some have the attitude, "I'm a person and that's a bear. Get it out of here." Still shakes his head and counters this attitude with his own: "If they're going to live in bear territory, they have to learn to live with the bears. They were here first." Ironically, people don't always want to accommodate nature, while "they'll live right in the middle of it." The bottom line, says Still, is that if you "don't have an attractant, the bears will leave." However, occasionally a bear becomes an actual nuisance, and one of Still's odious tasks as a bear biologist was to kill any that fell into that category. For example, if a bear enters a dwelling, it has to be killed. Once he had to dispatch a bear that opened the door to a mudroom just as a woman opened another, scaring each other to death. The idea is that if a bear will enter a human habitation, it has lost its fear and could possibly pose a physical threat. That said, no bear-related human fatalities have ever documented in South Carolina. In fact, only three deaths by black bears have been recorded on the East Coast: two in Tennessee and one in New York. In one of the incidents in Tennessee, the circumstances are not known; in the other, the bear had just come out of hibernation, was surprised a group of people and attacked them when they ran away, probably triggering the hungry bear's prey drive; in New York, a young child who was covered in spilled milk tragically was killed by a bear that probably was attracted by the smell.

On the extreme chance a black bear attacks you, Still has advice. First, overcome your instinct to run, because then you become prey. Once the drive is triggered, the bear usually follows through. Don't climb a tree. Make yourself as big as possible. Face the bear but don't make direct eye contact, which can be interpreted as a challenge. Make noise, increasing gradually in volume. Wave your hands around. If the bear charges, throw rocks. In the very unlikely case the bear attacks, fight back, going for the eyes, nose and reproductive organs. Again, though, a black bear probably won't attack you, reiterates Still. The only injury he knows of occurred when a biology graduate student was helping trap bears and a freshly released one charged by him and nipped him on the rear end while fleeing the scene.

Ironically, bear hunting is one reason the bear population is booming. In the early 2000s, the SC DNR wrote a bill, supported by ForestWatch and the Bear Hunters' Association, that increased the penalty for killing a bear out of season to a $2,500 fine, $2,500 in restitution, seizure of vehicle and revocation of hunting license. The action stalled the practice of killing bears for their gallbladders, a wasteful and abominable practice based on the (mostly Chinese) myth that consuming this organ increases male vitality. Simultaneously, Still supposes, the bear population "hit a threshold and took off." Hunting a bear, says Still, is not like "shooting a refrigerator

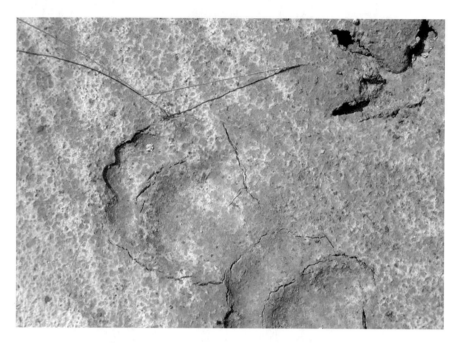

Bear track. In the upper right corner is a turkey track. *Photo by Skip Still.*

out of a tree," as some people are said to think. A lot happens before you even get him to climb one. You need good tracking dogs, and you have to be able to follow them over and through the steep, brush-covered terrain. "You might not even see the bear," he remarks. Still is pro–bear hunting for two reasons: the tradition behind it; and "It puts the fear of man, and dog, in a bear." A bear that fears humans and dogs is generally a bear that stays out of trouble.

The Chattooga River watershed is a good place for bears, due to the mild climate and the diversity of (natural) food. Being opportunistic omnivores, bears will gormandize not only acorns, berries and fruit but also buds, bark, grass and just about anything digestible. The sighting of a bear in the woods seldom happens but never is forgotten. The saucer-eyed look of surprise and the snort of alarm engender not fear but awe, and the thrill of seeing a charismatic mammal in its natural habitat is singular and priceless. "Bears can learn to live with humans," says Still. "The question is, can humans learn to live with bears?" Let's hope so.

Echoes of the Past

The Oconee Heritage Center (OHC) is as rich and variable as the history it showcases. In the front room, a display shelf holds an old banjo and a fiddle from the 1930s, symbols of a time when music was one of the few entertainments available. The instruments also hint at their countries of origin: the banjo came over with slaves from Africa; fiddles from Ireland and Scotland were brought to the Appalachian Mountains and used to morph Celtic music into bluegrass. A sweet potato the size of a football rests on a table next to a loofa made from another African import, a type of okra. Cookbooks, historical narratives and volumes of ghost stories are arranged on a shelf next to CDs of old-time music, South Carolina memorabilia and jewelry, jars of chow-chow and homemade soap. Free brochures feature local sights and activities for tourists.

Perhaps the most curious display is one of hundreds of salt-and-pepper shakers bequeathed by a local widow. The receptacles represent her travels and include South Carolina peaches, dancing hippos, black-and-white chickens, Coke and Pepsi bottles, blackface characters, rainbow trout, Texas cowboy hats, bespectacled owls and two clamshells fashioned into toilets (for salt and pepper dispersal!) with the help of old-fashioned beer tabs. They are a poignant attempt at mortality, a reminder that all is vanity. Collect salt-and-pepper shakers or money, in the end, leave it all behind in a display case or someone else's pockets.

The centerpiece of the museum is a 250-year-old canoe, which was found in the Chattooga River in 2002 by Peter Peteet. He was swimming in the river one day when he noticed something that, at first glance, looked like a bit of driftwood sticking out of a bank. After a bit of excavation and closer inspection, Peteet suspected that it was something more, and he was right. He had unearthed a thirty-two-foot pirogue, a canoe made of yellow pine. While it was constructed in the manner of the Cherokee, the iron tools of white settlers were used, so its origins are uncertain. The canoe was almost completely buried and submerged about a mile downstream of Earl's Ford, a crossing point on a Cherokee travel route, where it probably was used as a ferry. Peteet contacted authorities, but the issue of excavation was complicated by the fact that the canoe was located in the river, which is the dividing line between South Carolina and Georgia and therefore under the jurisdiction of two national forest regional offices. After two years of governmental equivocation, word was getting out on the Internet about the historical artifact, inspiring fear that the canoe would be stolen or vandalized. In response, Buzz Williams of the Chattooga Conservancy directed an effort to retrieve the canoe and move it to the Oconee Heritage Center, located in Walhalla, South Carolina.

The tour of the center is self-guided and winds through a corridor from past to present. Old farm implements and display cases of musket balls and tools line one wall, and on another are portraits and notecards describing notable people who visited the area. Andre Michaux, born in 1746 in France, led a scientific expedition in 1785 for the French government. His objective was to find new species of timber for his country, which had depleted its own after protracted warfare with the British. He traveled to Charleston in 1786, along the way introducing such plants as the mimosa, the camellia and the crepe myrtle. (He obviously didn't know about the danger of importing nonnative species.) During his trip up the Savannah River, he discovered the Oconee bell and also named 293 new species of plants to the area, which he visited seven times. Unfortunately, on his trip home in 1796, his ship wrecked and he lost most of the plants he had collected. Later, an American botanist realized that classification of the Oconee bell had somehow been overlooked and traveled to the region to try to rediscover it. He failed, and for fifty years the plant remained elusive. Finally, in 1887, a seventeen-year-old boy, George Hyams, rediscovered the legendary wildflower endemic to the gorges of the Blue Ridge Escarpment.

Another significant person to visit the area was Andrew Ellicott, who in 1811 was charged by the State of Georgia with finding the boundary between it and North Carolina. He discovered that the line actually was eighteen miles farther south than originally believed, depriving Georgia of some real estate; in reward for his yearlong effort, the state petulantly refused Ellicott full payment. In 1813, commissioners from North Carolina and South Carolina agreed to designate Ellicott's Rock in the Chattooga River as the boundary. The rock, inscribed "Latitude 35/AD 1813/ NC+SC," now is considered to mark where Georgia, North Carolina and South Carolina meet and is on the National Register of Historic Places. Despite the fact that Ellicott did not make the insignia, the rock was named after him, perhaps in belated regret for his shortchange. In 1975, 8,274 acres in the vicinity were designated Ellicott Rock Wilderness. The Chattooga River runs right through this wilderness area, the only one in the country that lies in three states.

The famous naturalist William Bartram is represented here also. In 1773, he began his *Travels* (1791), which describe his observations of plants on his rambles through North Carolina, South Carolina, Georgia and other parts of the South. He had a deep appreciation for the botanical bounty that awaited him, saying, "The temperate zone...exhibits scenes of infinitely greater variety, magnificence and consequence," foreshadowing what biologists now know about the incredible diversity of the area. After climbing "Occonne [*sic*] mountain," he describes the view of the undulating landscape to "the great ocean after a tempest" and later crosses "a delightful river, the main branch of the Tugilo [*sic*]": the Chattooga. Bartram, who copiously catalogued everything he encountered, discovered the Franklin tree, now extinct in the wild. His peregrinations are memorialized by a hiking trail that follows his route, which runs 220 miles from northeast Georgia to the Savannah River in Augusta. Modern obstacles obstruct parts of the Bartram Trail; however, 37 miles wind through the mountains, merging briefly with both the Foothills Trail and the Chattooga River Trail to run alongside the river for about 10 miles.

Another famous landmark is, or rather was, the Russell House, located in a fertile hollow embraced by the Chattooga. The house, which mysteriously burned in 1988, was the only stopover on the trip from Walhalla to Highlands, North Carolina. A thirty-mile trip that takes forty-five minutes by car, in stagecoach days it was a two-day event. The house was built in 1867 by Ganaway Russell and included several outbuildings, some of which still stand. The site, which is slowly being swallowed by the forest, is on the National Register of Historic Places and has another, older significance: a Cherokee village once stood in the field behind the house.

In 1989, anthropology professor Gerald Schroedl of the University of Tennessee began investigating the site, which is thought to be the only

Cherokee town in the Chattooga River watershed. "We're not sure how the site was discovered," says Schroedl, although he thinks it first was recorded by the Forest Service in the 1960s and speculates that local people have known about it for a long time. The site of Chattooga Town probably was the only suitable location for a village, as it was the only bottomland right next to the river. Because of the size and location of the space, the Cherokee had rich bottomland soil on which to grow corn, as well as the room to grow it, build a village and sustain everything. Ten to twelve domestic houses and a town house were discovered on the site, unusual because the Cherokee usually did not build a town house or recognize a town as such unless it had at least one hundred dwellings. "This was an out-of-the-way place, a sleepy village with about five or ten families who had a fully functioning town," Schroedl observes. Among their activities were making soapstone pipes, he believes, and trading with other Cherokees and with white settlers, although the dig did not produce the quantities of trade goods found in other Cherokee towns. Not surprising, since Cherokee Town was hard to access in its nook at the bottom of an isolated mountain valley. The town was abandoned around 1730 for reasons unknown but suspected: possibly hostile incursions by the nearby Creek people or perhaps an outbreak of smallpox. As Schroedl points out, Chattooga Town "was almost not a town," meaning that it would take only the loss of a few of its inhabitants to make living there unsustainable. Schroedl finished his work there in 1994, and the site is now a green field where once a small band of Cherokee lived, farming their crops, making pipes and carrying on the business of living.

According to "The History of the Andrew Pickens Ranger Station," by the mid-1700s, white settlers had begun their encroachment into Cherokee territory. The settlers traded with the British, who also posted soldiers there to protect their interests. In the so-called Cherokee wars (1759–61), the Indians launched a series of attacks on the settlers. As was the case so often, they were summarily crushed; in 1760, a British expedition wiped out most of the Cherokee villages. While some Indians rebuilt, many moved farther west to avoid further conflict. Those who stayed were destroyed once again, this time by Americans, during the American Revolution; for some reason, the Indians had taken sides with the British. After the war, white settlers began moving in again to start small farms. Many of these were located along the banks of streams, including the Chattooga, and produced crops and livestock. In 1852, an attempt was made to construct a railroad across the mountains from West Union, near Walhalla, through Georgia and into Tennessee. The effort failed due to financial reasons, but the beginnings of a

Excavating the Cherokee town house at Chattooga Town. *Photo by Gerald Schroedl.*

one-mile tunnel can be found at Stumphouse Mountain, located about two miles south of the ranger station. The tunnel was later used to ferment blue cheese made by agricultural institution Clemson College, now a university. During the late 1800s and early 1900s, extensive logging destroyed most of the old-growth forest in the area. The Weeks Act authorized the purchase of land in the Savannah Purchase Unit, establishing the General Pickens District in 1914; in 1936, the district became part of the Sumter National Forest, and by the 1940s, they had procured "the extensive cutover lands of the Whitewater River Lumber Company." Since then, the Forest Service has applied conservation efforts to "restore the productivity and health of the forest." In the 1930s, the Civilian Conservation Corps helped the agency construct campgrounds, trails, picnic areas and the fish hatchery.

Leslie White is the director and curator of the OHC, which opened in 2004. "Our mission is to preserve and promote the cultural history of Oconee County," she says. Most of the artifacts in the museum were donated, and 50 percent of its funding comes from the county, with the rest from grants, fundraisers and donations. She stands next to a display case containing *Deliverance* memorabilia, including an album of "Dueling Banjos" and a 1983 edition of *National Geographic* featuring an article about the actual people of these mountains, rural farmers and those involved in what some consider a questionable activity: making moonshine. White, who was raised in Walhalla, says she's sure people still operate stills in the mountains. In fact, she recently saw a suspected moonshiner in the grocery store. "He had a huge bag of sugar," she says meaningfully.

The walk through time continues past a Confederate uniform standing at permanent attention before a Confederate flag. A big basket full of cotton bolls conjures a vision of the crop being picked by slaves, without whom this commodity would not have been viable. Alongside it rest other remnants of the past, including a chamber pot and a liquor distillery. The walk concludes with a full radiation protection suit displayed beside photographs depicting the construction of dams erected by Duke Energy to provide hydroelectric power for the area.

Long after the tour is over, images of the past remain fixed in memory, along with a sense of wonder at the changes wrought by time and man. From a handcrafted wooden canoe to nuclear fission in just 250 of 10,000 years of human history, the question begs: "What's next?" Meanwhile, the river flows.

Watchers of the Forest

N onprofits and people who volunteer are exactly what we need to change the world," says Wayne Jenkins, who served for more than seven years as executive director of Georgia ForestWatch. In the past twenty-plus years, this nonprofit environmental organization has changed the world—at least the one in its own backyard. The group began in 1986 as a coalition of seven conservation groups that joined forces in an effort to demand input and transparency from the Forest Service. As Jenkins puts it, "ForestWatch was a reaction to rampant road building and clear cutting and the effects that those had on the Chattahoochee-Oconee National Forests in Georgia," part of the Chattooga River watershed. The organization eventually helped stop what it deemed these destructive practices and tried to define a new model for restoring and harvesting trees.

Restoration is an important concept because if you use up something and don't replace it, then you eventually run out of it. However, in the case of the Forest Service, habitat restoration traditionally has consisted of planting an entirely different tree—the pine—than the hardwoods that have been logged out. "Hardwood restoration is not rocket science," as Jenkins half jokes. "It's more complicated." The original landscape, he explains, was ancient, with complex forest types existing on differing elevations. The chestnut blight changed the complexion of the Appalachian Mountain range when it wiped out the American chestnut tree in the twentieth century; at the same time, the first industrial harvesting was occurring and continued until most of the old growth was logged out. When the sawdust settled and the loggers left,

Loggers removed most of the old-growth forest from the Chattooga River watershed in the nineteenth century. *Courtesy of Great Smoky Mountains National Park Library.*

second growth began. About this time, the Forest Service came into being and started managing and restoring the forest. "But restore to what?" asks Jenkins. As he points out, most foresters were "raised on pine and spruce," so that's what they wanted to plant. Of course, it's convenient that these trees grow fast and are ready sooner than hardwoods to be sold as timber. The point is that these mountain forests were not originally constituted of pine and so to properly restore them means to replant hardwoods.

When hardwoods are (rightfully) restored, however, the whole paradigm of management has to change because hardwoods take so much longer to grow and reach harvesting size. Jenkins, who is not opposed to cutting trees "the right way," explains, "Forestry is all about 50-, 100-, 150-, 200-year horizons." (Don't go into forestry if you crave instant gratification.) Instead of logging entire swaths, as with pine, hardwood cuts must reflect natural disturbances, which are small scale and "happening across the landscape on nature's timeline." Openings caused by fallen old-growth trees typically measure about a half acre. These small-scale disturbances happen continuously to "drive a hardwood forest and create the diversity of species that we associate with those natural hardwoods. You got this shifting diversity moving across the landscape all the time within the range of certain mixes of trees based on elevation, aspect, soil type, moisture regime, an unbelievably beautiful and complicated system," he continues. Imagine a large tree shading smaller trees. During an intense storm, the large tree is knocked over, creating a gap through which sun can shine on the smaller trees. These small trees grow larger, fed by the light and the nutrients in the soil that are enriched by the decay of the fallen tree. In this way, the cycle continues: the trees not only feed the forest by recycling back into the soil but also shade creeks, drop mast for wildlife and provide shelter for birds and small mammals. These relationships have developed, slowly, over eons; if one crucial factor is changed, the whole dynamic is disrupted. Certain types of wildlife that need hardwoods cannot live in pine forests, for example. Deer need acorns, not pine needles. "If you want to keep the natural regime and the diversity, you have to mimic the disturbance regime," Jenkins says. In a hardwood forest, this calls for selective cutting, something the Forest Service didn't practice historically.

What the agency did do was cut trees and build roads into the woods in order to reach the trees and harvest them. But times they were a-changin' in 1976, when the Forest Service was ordered to "curtail clear-cutting, provide for biological diversity, protect streams and water quality, limit uneconomic timbering and provide public input" by the National Forest Management Act. Part of this federal mandate charged the Forest Service to develop a management plan for Georgia's Chattahoochee-Oconee National Forest and its resources. The result, in 1984, was the "Land and Resource Management Plan," prepared by the Forest Service; however, the plan ignored the directive to obtain public input, according to a Georgia ForestWatch report, "Our History." Furthermore, the public was given only sixty days to read and respond to the 750-page draft, which had taken years to write. A conservation coalition—made up of the Georgia Conservancy, the Wilderness Society, the Sierra Club, Friends of the Mountains, Georgia Botanical Society, Atlanta Audubon Society and the Georgia Council of Trout Unlimited—asked for and received a ninety-day extension.

The groups also hired consultants and a lawyer to assist with deconstructing the Forest Service's plan. However, as they slogged through the treatise, differences arose over priorities. Some considered logging the biggest concern, while others wanted to focus on wildlife or botanical issues. Fear surfaced that "'the big three'—the Georgia Conservancy, Sierra Club and The Wilderness Society—would dictate the final response to the Forest Service," according to the ForestWatch report. The groups diverged over the disagreements and filed separate comments with the Forest Service; however, they did concur that the draft plan called for excessive logging, clear-cutting, road building and herbicide use. All of the splinter groups managed to submit their comments but "only a few minutes before midnight of the final day." In its turn, the Forest Service was overwhelmed with public comment, receiving more than two thousand missives about the proposed plan. Despite the flood of feedback, the agency's final draft for the 1985 Chattahoochee-Oconee National Forests was almost identical to the first. "Disappointment was profound," and the coalition feared that the forests would be vulnerable if the plan was implemented as written. The public had forty-five days to file appeals, and members of the coalition rejoined forces.

At this point, worried that the appeal would set "a national precedent that would jeopardize management plans for other national forests," the Forest Service offered to negotiate a settlement. Terms called for the Forest Service to meet annually with coalition members, to submit to ground-level surveillance by them and to disclose plans for logging and other activities. At this point, the coalition coalesced into the Georgia ForestWatch, and in 1986, organization volunteers paired with Forest Service rangers on their first monitoring venture.

The Forest Service is charged with the protection of watersheds, fish and wildlife habitat, scenic beauty, wilderness and recreation in the national forests; however, logging also is a part of its mission and can affect soil, wildlife, water and fish and scenery. When interests compete, usually the moneymaking one (for instance, logging) wins out at the expense of the other (for instance, protection of a watershed from the runoff of sediment). ForestWatch was committed to defending the interests of the entire forest, making sure that one interest would not win out over another based on monetary value. Along those lines, volunteers monitored the Forest Service, meeting annually with the agency to review any proposed plans, such as timber sales or road-building projects. In 1991, two discoveries illustrated why such oversight was necessary, according to ForestWatch. First, an endangered species of orchid was found by a ForestWatch volunteer in an area slated for timber harvesting by the Forest Service, which, as a result, cancelled the sale. Second, the discovery of the orchid by outside sources revealed that the Forest Service was not following the federal mandate to conduct environmental surveys of proposed logging areas, which is why the agency did not find the endangered plant.

A Natural and Cultural History

By the time ForestWatch had incorporated and become a nonprofit organization, the Forest Service had begun to push back against pressure to reduce timber sales as more and more acres of wilderness were protected against logging. Relations between the two groups finally degenerated to the point that the Forest Service ended its annual meetings with ForestWatch and announced that henceforth, it would disclose its proposed logging projects only through the legally required channels. In addition, the agency instituted tougher rules for filing appeals, perhaps an effort to erode the efficacy of organizations like ForestWatch.

Another challenge loomed in the early 1990s when the Forest Service began developing a new "Forest Land and Resource Management Plan" for the Chattahoochee-Oconee National Park. As the ForestWatch report puts it, "After nearly a century of re-growth, [southern forests] were ripe for the chainsaw," and the Forest Service was laying plans to log the region. In response, ForestWatch began a defensive move to protect "the natural splendor and ecological integrity of Georgia's national forests." The result was an eighty-page booklet entitled *Georgia's Mountain Treasures: The Unprotected Wildlands of the Chattahoochee-Oconee National Forests*. The report was one of three published by the Wilderness Society; the other two addressed the Nantahala and Pisgah National Forests in North Carolina and the Andrew Pickens District of the Sumter National Forest in South Carolina. Fourteen environmental groups contributed to the report, which was endorsed by former president Jimmy Carter and requested that forty-four wild areas comprising 235,700 acres be protected from logging and road building.

The report requested that the Forest Service withhold from logging in the area, home to pockets of old growth, trout streams and wildlife habitat, until the agency could consider ForestWatch's plan. The answer was a resounding "No" because, according to ForestWatch, the Forest Service was under pressure from the timber industry. However, the Forest Service was required to solicit public comment about its proposed uses for the area, but as the agency proceeded and time passed, ForestWatch managed to garner support for its plan, reporting that "public input during the early comment period of the process was the largest for any forest in the Southeast." Through this and several other legal challenges, ForestWatch was able to halt all timber sales in the Chattahoochee-Oconee National Forest by 1996.

In 1998, ForestWatch installed its first executive director, Brent Martin. Challenges continued to arise. One was the documentation of hundreds of miles of illegal ATV trails that had severely damaged the forest and the ensuing defeat of legislation that would have legalized ATVs on gravel roads and made their use harder to regulate. In addition, volunteers documented eleven thousand acres of old growth, which the Forest Service had denied existed, according to ForestWatch, and Martin hired an aquatic biologist to give the organization more scientific credibility. After a decade of vigorous growth and activity, ForestWatch faced a crisis when funds and support started dwindling and staffers—including Martin—moved on. ForestWatch almost dissolved but at the last minute pulled itself together and continued its work. Wayne Jenkins, installed as the new executive director, restored confidence in the organization. His efforts included obtaining financial support for the University of Georgia's predator insect lab, charged with finding ways to combat the wooly adelgid devastating the eastern hemlock; and collaborating with Forest Service agents in the development of a new forest plan, one that focuses on restoration as opposed to timber production.

As long as the forest exists, people will fight over how it is to be used and to what extent. In the case of the Chattooga River watershed, the outcome seems more important due to the fact that this place is so special. However, not everyone believes that something should be allowed to simply exist; its value lies in how it can be exploited for economic gain. For this reason, Georgia ForestWatch stands ready to protect these woods and the river running through it.

A Day in Court

What does the future hold for the Chattooga River? No one knows. The following account offers a preview of the kinds of disagreements that might arise as people attempt to define their own, often disparate, ideas about how the resource should be used. The drama unfolds in a courthouse in South Carolina, in a city far from the banks of the river at the center of the dispute.

A dozen or so people, mostly youngish men, mill around in front of the doors to the courtroom waiting for the legal arguments to begin. Several introduce themselves as paddlers, seeming slightly ill at ease in suits and ties. "I've never seen you so dressed up," exclaims one to another. While none is being called on for testimony, they clearly want to make a good impression. On the other hand, environmental activist Buzz Williams wears a faded sweatshirt, blue jeans and well-worn leather boots. "I may even have some manure on 'em," he cracks, perhaps reflecting his opinion concerning the proceedings.

The issue before a U.S. District Court is whether the Forest Service can ban and/or severely limit paddling on the Chattooga River. The players are American Whitewater (AW) on one side; on the other, the Forest Service, the Rust family and Georgia ForestWatch, which are working together against AW. As if things aren't confusing enough, the Rust family and Georgia ForestWatch both are challenging the Forest Service—just not at this particular time.

The following is a summary and does not attempt to offer a detailed account of events, which started decades ago and are as turbulent as white water. Over the years, thousands of pieces of paper milled from countless trees have conveyed rivers of words over the issue; an additional book would be needed to explain it all. In this case, twenty-seven thousand pages of documents are being used to decide the case, says Kevin Colburn, national stewardship director of AW. Colburn discussed the issue at length, from Montana, in a telephone interview.

Paddlers long desired access to the entire Chattooga, but since 1976, they have been restricted to the area below the Highway 28 Bridge, constituting thirty-three miles. In 2012, under longtime and intense pressure from AW, the Washington Office of the U.S. Forest Service opened seventeen of the upper Chattooga's twenty-four miles from December to April, and with certain restrictions. However, according to AW, the management plan for the river included "unfair and illegal prohibitions and limits on paddling." The group now seeks to run the entire river without any restrictions, at any time of the year and at any water level. In 2001, AW began an earnest campaign to secure boating rights to the upper Chattooga with a request to the Forest Service, which was declined. Thus began a protracted battle in which the Forest Service stumbled and stonewalled and the AW launched attack after attack in an attempt to gain its objective. Among AW's allegations were that the Forest Service never offered sufficient evidence that a boating ban was necessary and that the ban violated several federal laws, including the Wilderness Act and the Wild and Scenic Rivers Act.

American Whitewater is a nonprofit organization whose mission statement is "to conserve and restore America's whitewater resources and to enhance opportunities to enjoy them safely." The organization has worked on behalf of river conservation and restoration since its inception in 1954 and has assisted government and private agencies in the removal of dams. In addition, AW helped found the Outdoor Alliance, which has "a long tradition of preserving public access to America's Outdoors—making sure people have trails to hike, waters to paddle, mountains to ski and crags to climb." In other words, the organization is about access, as well as protection, asserting in its suit that the ban violates the Wilderness Act and the Wild and Scenic River Act, which reads in part that the river must be preserved for "the benefit and enjoyment" of its "recreational values." However, five miles of the disputed section of the Chattooga pass through the Ellicott Rock Wilderness, and opening up this part of the river "would encourage use creation of put-ins, take-outs and approach trails," causing damage to the riverbank and the potentially sensitive flora growing there, according to Buzz Williams, founder of the Chattooga Conservancy.

Many years, reports, amendments to reports, letters, user analyses and environmental assessments later, the case sits before a judge who will decide the outcome. First up, the plaintiffs: American Whitewater, on behalf of paddlers. The AW lawyer—let's call him Tom—seems relaxed, as though he takes for granted that people will listen to him. Imagine him in a T-shirt and jeans, instead of a suit and tie, and he could be a frat boy. His first tactic is to show the judge a short video, "by way of demonstration," taken recently on the upper section of the river. "What the plaintiffs are asking for is normalcy," he states, adding that no other Wild and Scenic River has boating restrictions in place, an assertion that the Forest Service later claims is a fallacy. "Maybe they decided it was time," retorts the judge, who throughout the hearing demonstrates a firm grasp of the issue. About forty-five, an attractive blond with razor focus, she frequently interrupts Tom with questions and comments. The conversation quickly narrows to whether or not boating should be considered an "ORV," or outstanding remarkable value, one of the criteria used to describe a Wild and Scenic River. Brandishing a copy of the Forest Service's "Wild and Scenic River Study," Tom insists, "Boating was a reason the Chattooga River was designated a Wild and Scenic River." However, some people estimate that only 150 or so people used the river annually for boating prior to its Wild and Scenic status. Currently, tens of thousands do so.

The judge repeatedly asks Tom precisely where in the study boating was listed as an ORV, stating, "If Congress didn't designate it, I can't." She wonders about other ORVs, which include scenery, geology, fish and wildlife, history and culture, and suggests at one point that boating is a component of the "recreation" ORV, as opposed to a distinct ORV. Interestingly, while attempting to uphold his view that boating is in fact a separate ORV, Tom seems to dismiss three others—scenery, fish and wildlife—saying, "There's nothing special about biology." He ultimately alleges that the Forest Service never provided evidence that boating on the upper Chattooga would conflict with other uses, such as fishing; that the agency never conducted a proper environmental assessment of the area to show what impacts, if any, would result from boating activities; and that the Forest Service used its own illegal regulations to support its present position on restrictions. Buzz Williams, sitting in the front row of the gallery, grumbles, "So far no one's mentioned 'solitude' one time," referring to another ORV that is hard to quantify.

After Tom concludes, the lawyer for the Forest Service faces the judge. Nervous almost to the point of twitchiness, he talks so fast that the court reporter has to ask him four times to slow down. Redheaded, with closely cropped facial hair, he looks adolescent—like a bearded twelve-year-old. We'll call him Dick; however, his testimony will not be summarized because he was virtually impossible to understand. Suffice to say that he tried to explain to the judge why the Forest Service should be able to set regulations on the river. The Forest Service, later contacted for comment and/or clarification, refused to discuss the issue.

The next lawyer for the defendants, "Harry," is poised, pleasant and marble-mouthed. He pronounces "river" as though it begins with three "R"s and ends with "ah": "Rrrivah." He would look perfectly at home in the South in 1950, or 1850, in a blue seersucker suit and bow tie, mint julep in hand. He argues for the Rust family, who has owned property along the banks of the upper Chattooga for sixty years. With a video of his own, he proceeds to illustrate why the stretch is non-navigable: a thin skin of water trickles over a rock as a plastic yellow ducky struggles to slide down it.

Harry then launches into his argument, which concerns but is not aimed directly at AW; he asserts that the Forest Service, in its decision to allow boating in the upper section, didn't address the impact of new access trails that will have to be built so that boaters can reach the river. He contends that the Forest Service violates its own regulations when officials say they will do an environmental impact study "later"—in other words, after the impact is felt. After the horse has absconded from the barn, so to speak. Harry also states that the Rust family has suffered harm from the decision to allow boating. The judge asks him to elaborate, and he informs her that littering has occurred and "No Trespassing" signs have been torn down. He also expresses concerns that, if allowed to use that part of the river, people might "come to think of it [the Rust property] as public" and that the family does not want the entailed risk of liability. The Rust family also declined to discuss the case for legal reasons, and evidence suggests that the family has taken steps to prevent boating on the section of the river that runs through their property. During a telephone interview, Colburn reported that the Rusts had erected barriers, of which he provided a photograph.

Next up is a ForestWatch lawyer. Thirty-something, with long, curly hair barely contained in a bun at the nape of her neck, "Jane" calmly and confidently offers arguments against boating on the upper Chattooga. She alleges that the Forest Service has violated the Wilderness Act, "one of the most lyrical pieces of prose in government writing," which reads in part: "A wilderness, in contrast with those areas where man and his own works dominate the landscape, is hereby recognized as an area where the earth and community of life are untrammeled by man, where man himself is a visitor who does not remain." In a telephone interview, Jane says she is concerned that the Forest Service will be unable to sufficiently monitor activity on and around the river. Because the Chattooga is monitored by three Forest Service offices located in three different states, no comprehensive management plan exists. "The Forest Service simply doesn't have the resources to dedicate to the monitoring, adaptive management and enforcement that it said it would do," she explains.

Next come counterarguments, given first by, for some reason, a different AW lawyer. Sounding slightly petulant, he says, somewhat pointlessly, "There are days when the water levels are so low they [boaters] wouldn't even want to be on the river." His voice is soft yet clipped, hard to hear even though he speaks into a microphone. Dick from the Forest Service speaks next, commenting, "No one's going to get everything they want." Possibly, no one is going to get anything; or, perhaps, everyone is going to get nothing, if the process continues to be hampered by flawed documents and protracted bouts of litigation. Plenty of evidence exists to suggest an inattention to detail, if not incompetence, on behalf of some parties.

Harry, lawyer for the Rust family, reiterates that the Forest Service should have assessed how use on the upper Chattooga would affect the property, and since it did not, the decision to allow boating—restricted or otherwise—is invalid. Jane from ForestWatch recaps her points. Then each lawyer makes closing remarks, during which the Forest Service tries to one-up the AW by pointing out that some Wild and Scenic Rivers do in fact have boating restrictions, trying to crack the foundation of Tom's assertion that none do. (Later, via phone, AW's Colburn explains that while boating restrictions are on the books for that river, located out West, they aren't enforced.) After four long hours punctuated by a couple of breaks, it's over, and everyone staggers exhaustedly to their cars.

The good news, at least to Williams and the Chattooga Conservancy's lawyer, Andy Smith, is that the Forest Service's "failure to comply with its own regulations" opens up a legal avenue for the Chattooga Conservancy. Both Williams and Smith are former river guides; Smith quips that his job on the river paid for law school. In fact, he looks more river rat than lawyer. His curly, gray-flecked brown hair spills over the collar of his shirt, and he sports an attractive, thriving crop of facial hair, as opposed to the quasi beard in vogue at the time of this writing. His hands, large, brown and weathered, look like they spend more time chopping wood than filing briefs.

Williams hopes to prevent boating on the upper part of the river because the area is "the last little beating heart of wildness" in the watershed and "the most biologically rich and still unused place on the Chattooga." He worries about the effect of two proposed trails that would lead boaters to and from the river. He points out that once trails are constructed into the area, not only boaters but also birdwatchers, hikers, photographers and sightseers will likely want to explore it, causing further degradation of the "biology" ORV.

Before the matter became a legal issue, the Georgia Chapter of the Sierra Club, Wilderness Watch and the Chattooga Conservancy were participating in the discussion with the Forest Service, American Whitewater and others in the hope of consensus. According to Williams, the Chattooga Conservancy was the only group that offered a compromise: for boaters to give up the waters between Grimshaw's Bridge and Bull Pen Bridge, part of the disputed area and the portion comprising the most biologically sensitive area. It runs through a gorge and is virtually non-navigable anyway, he adds. "Most of the paddlers I know agreed" to this compromise, says Williams. "You don't stop anyone from using the resource, but you have to restrict access in order to protect it," he adds. Clearly, when the act was written its authors did not foresee how anyone could perceive a conflict between one use and another. The point is moot, anyway, since Williams and the conservancy are not involved. This time.

The court eventually ruled that the Forest Service has the discretion to restrict boating and upheld the current policy allowing restricted paddling on the upper Chattooga from December through April. In a press release, AW called the decision a disappointment yet also a victory for the paddling community and said that the organization is "evaluating the legal options, but regardless will continue to work with the Forest Service to bring responsible and nationally consistent river management to the Upper Chattooga." Meanwhile, the river continues to run, chattering to itself and heedless of the human drama unfolding around it.

Sources

American Whitewater. "American Whitewater Chattooga Project." www. americanwhitewater.org/content/Project/view/id/chattooga.

————. "Chattooga USFS Consideration Done—River to Partially Open This Winter." www.americanwhitewater.org/content/Article/view/articleid/31480.

————. "Timeline of Critical Actions." www.americanwhitewater.org/content/Wiki/aw:chattooga_history.

Bat Conservation International. www.batcon.org.

Boorman, John. "*Deliverance* Deluxe Edition DVD with Interviews." Warner Video, 2000.

Boyd, Brian. *The Chattooga Wild and Scenic River.* Clayton, GA: Fern Creek Press, 1993.

Brown's Guide to Georgia. "Chattooga River Hiking Trail." www. brownsguides.com/blog/chattooga-river-hiking-trail.

Centers for Disease Control. "Human Rabies." www.cdc.gov/rabies/index.html.

Chattahoochee-Oconee National Forest. "About the Forest." www.fs.usda. gov/main/conf/about-forest.

The Chattooga Conservancy. "Mission and Goals." www.chattoogariver. org/?page_id=67.

"Chattooga River Fatalities and Near Fatalities Since 1970." United States Forest Service, 2012.

Chattooga River Wild and Scenic River. "Chattooga River & Tributaries." chattooga-river.net.

SOURCES

Clay, Butch. *A Guide to the Chattooga River*. Birmingham, AL: Chattooga River Publishing, 1995.

Clemson Cooperative Extension. "South Carolina Wild Hog Task Force." www.clemson.edu/extension/natural_resources/wildlife/wildhogs.

The Conservation Ethics Group. "What Is Conservation Ethics?" www.conservationethics.org.

Cooperative Extension System. "Imported Fire Ant History." www.extension.org/pages/11051/imported-fire-ant-history.

Cox, Ronny. *Dueling Banjos: The Deliverance of Drew*. Cleveland, OH: Felsen Press, 2012.

Dallmeyer, Dorothy. *William Bartram's Living Legacy: The Travels and the Nature of the South*. Macon, GA: Mercer University Press, 2010.

Davis, Richard C., ed. *The Encyclopedia of American Forest and Conservation History*. New York: Macmillan, 1983. Vol. 2, 685.

Dickey, James. *Deliverance*. New York: Dell Publishing Company, 1970.

Don't Move Firewood. "The Problem." www.dontmovefirewood.org/the-problem.html.

Erwin, T.L. "The Biodiversity Question: How Many Species of Terrestrial Arthropods Are There?" In *Forest Canopies, Second Edition*, edited by M.D. Lowman and H.B. Rinker, 259–69. Burlington, MA: Elsevier Academic Press, 2004.

Foothills Trail. www.foothillstrail.org.

Foottit, Robert G., and Peter H. Adler. *Insect Biodiversity: Science and Society*. Chichester, West Sussex, UK: Wiley and Blackwell, 2009.

Francis Marion and Sumter National Forests. "History of the Andrew Pickens Ranger District." www.fs.usda.gov/detail/scnfs/home/?cid=fsbdev3_037407.

Freinkel, Susan. *American Chestnut: The Life, Death, and Rebirth of a Perfect Tree*. Berkeley: University of California Press, 2007.

Gaddy, L.L. "Chick." *Spiders of the Carolinas*. Duluth, MN: Kollath+Stensaas Publishing, 2009.

Georgia College. "Crayfishes of Georgia." crayfishesofgeorgia.gcsu.edu.

Georgia ForestWatch. "Our History: 20 Years of Watching Your Forest." 2007.

Georgia Genealogy Trails. "Northeast Georgia Mountains: Indian Names of Places." genealogytrails.com/geo/nativeamer/indianplacenames.html.

GeorgiaTrails.com. "Bartram Trail." www.georgiatrails.com/gt/Bartram_Trail.

Hobbs, Horton H., Jr. *The Crayfishes of Georgia*. Washington, D.C.: Smithsonian Institution Press, 1981.

Sources

King, Thomas E. *Waterfall Hikes of Upstate South Carolina*. Greenville, SC: Keys Printing, 2005.

Lane, John. *Chattooga: Descending Into the Myth of Deliverance*. Athens: University of Georgia Press, 2004.

The Long Now: Revive and Restore. "The Great Passenger Pigeon Comeback." longnow.org/revive/projects.

Maclean, Norman. *A River Runs Through It*. Chicago: University of Chicago Press, 1976.

Minnesota Sea Grant. "Hyporthermia Prevention: Survival in Cold Water." seagrant.umn.edu/coastal_communities/hypothermia.

"National Forest Service Land Management Planning Rule." *Federal Register* 77, no. 68 (Monday, April 9, 2012): 21162–276.

National Forests in North Carolina. "Nantahala National Forest." www.fs.usda.gov/main/nfsnc/home.

National Park System: Great Smoky Mountains. "National Park Versus National Forest?" www.nps.gov/grsm/planyourvisit/np-versus-nf.htm.

National Wild and Scenic Rivers System. "About the WSR Act." www.rivers.gov/rivers/wsr-act.php.

———. "Chattooga River, Georgia, N. Carolina, S. Carolina." www.rivers.gov/rivers/rivers/chattooga.php.

———. "A National System." www.rivers.gov/rivers/national-system.php.

New Georgia Encyclopedia. "Land and Resources: American Chestnut." www.georgiaencyclopedia.org/nge/Article.jsp?id=h-944&hl=y.

New World Encyclopedia. "Crayfish." www.newworldencyclopedia.org/entry/Crayfish.

The Poetry Archive. "Mayflies," by Richard Wilbur. www.poetryarchive.org/poetryarchive/singlePoem.do?poemId=1673.

The Poetry Connection. "Dolor," by Theodore Roethke. www.poetryconnection.net/poets/Theodore_Roethke/4556.

South Carolina Department of Natural Resources. "Hunters: Help Control Coyotes and Save Our Deer!" www.dnr.sc.gov/wildlife/coyote/index.html.

———. "Wildlife—2012 Deer Record Information." www.dnr.sc.gov/wildlife/deer/2012DeerAntlerRecords.html.

South Carolina Trails Program. "Hiking Trail: Chattooga." www.sctrails.net/Trails/ALLTRAILS/Hiking/Upcountry/Chattooga.html.

Spauling, Heather, and Lynne K. Rieske. "The Aftermath of an Invasion: Structure and Composition of Central Appalachian Hemlock Forests Following Establishment of the Hemlock Wooly Adelgid, *Adelges tsugae*." *Biological Invasions* 12 (2010): 3135–43.

Sources

Trichoptera World Checklist. www.clemson.edu/cafls/departments/esps/database/trichopt.

United States Department of Agriculture. "Forest Service NEPA Projects." www.fs.fed.us/nepa/nepa_home.php.

United States Department of Agriculture/Forest Service. "Pest Alert: Wooly Adelgid." na.fs.fed.us/spfo/pubs/pest_al/hemlock/hwa05.htm.

United States Forest Service Francis Marion and Sumter National Forest. "History of the Andrew Pickens Ranger District." www.fs.usda.gov/detail/scnfs/home/?cid=fsbdev3_037407.

United States Geological Survey. "USGS Water Monthly Statistic for the Nation." waterdata.usgs.gov/usa/nwis/uv?site_no=02177000.

University of Rhode Island Landscape Horticulture Landscape Program. "Green Share Factsheet: Hemlock Woolly Adelgid." www.uri.edu/ce/factsheets/prints/hemadelgidprint.html.

Wilderness.net: The University of Montana. "Ellicott Rock Wilderness." www.wilderness.net/NWPS/wildView?wid=176.

———. "Frank Church." www.wilderness.net/NWPS/church.

YouTube. "Chattooga River Bull Sluice: Dude! Where's My Boat!" www.youtube.com/watch?v=ryQUfDQt7bQ.

Index

INDEX

Index

Index

About the Author

L aura Ann Garren was born in Clemson, South Carolina, not far from the Chattooga River. She holds two degrees from Clemson University: a bachelor's in English with a minor in wildlife biology and a master's in English with a concentration in environmental literature. She lives in Pendleton, South Carolina, with her husband, Chuck Linnell; dogs Rupert and Caper; and cat Rudy. In addition to being a writer, she cares for her husband, a stroke survivor; and is a certified dog trainer. Visit her website at www.LauraGarren. TheDogTrainer.org.

Photo by Heyward Douglass.

Visit us at
www.historypress.net

....

This title is also available as an e-book